the
Bridges of
Pittsburgh

by Bob Regan

photos by Tim Fabian

The Local History Company
publishers of history and heritage

Pittsburgh, Pennsylvania, USA

The Bridges of Pittsburgh
Copyright © 2006 by Bob Regan
Photographs by Tim Fabian

Published by
The Local History Company
112 North Woodland Road
Pittsburgh, PA 15232
www.TheLocalHistoryCompany.com
info@TheLocalHistoryCompany.com

The name "The Local History Company", "Publishers of History and Heritage", and its logo are trademarks of The Local History Company.

All maps are by the author.
Unless otherwise credited, all photos are by Tim Fabian. Front cover photo: Rachel Carson (9th Street) Bridge. Back cover photo: Downtown bridges along the Allegheny River.
Title page drawing of the Bigelow Boulevard Footbridge, courtesy of City of Pittsburgh Department of Public Works, Bureau of Engineering and Construction.

ISBN-13: 978-0-9770429-2-0
ISBN-10: 0-9770429-2-8

Library of Congress Cataloging-in-Publication Data

Regan, Bob, 1939-
    The Bridges of Pittsburgh / by Bob Regan ; photos by Tim Fabian.
        p.   cm.
    Includes bibliographical references and index. ISBN-13: 978-0-970429-2-0 (pbk.: alk. paper) ISBN-10: 0-9770429-2-8 (pbk.: alk. paper)
    1. Bridges—Pennsylvania—Pittsburgh. 2. Bridges—Pennsylvania—Pittsburgh—Guidebooks. 3. Pittsburgh (Pa.)—Description and travel. 4. Pittsburgh (Pa.)—Guidebooks. 5. Pittsburgh (Pa.)—Buildings, structures, etc. I. Title.

TG25.P59R44 2006
624.209748'86—dc22
                              2006009483

Printed in USA   1.5

D E D I C A T I O N

This book is formally dedicated to those hearty souls who conceived of, designed, and most importantly, built, the many bridges that adorn the city and make our lives a little easier.

And informally once again:

by Bob to

Zack, Brian, Alex, George, and now Lily and Ailey;

and by Tim to

Karen, Katrin, Leanna and Max for their love and support.

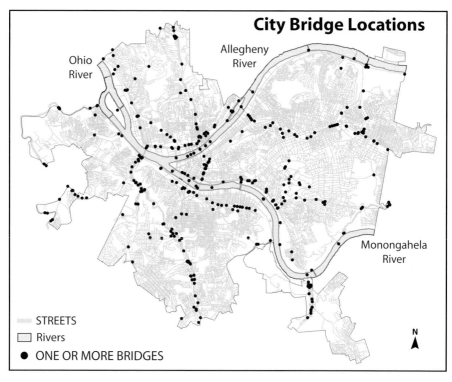

Map of the City of Pittsburgh showing the location of bridges within or at the city boundaries. Several of the bullets are the location of more than one bridge.

C O N T E N T S

ACKNOWLEDGMENTS

Mount Washington overlooking the Monongahela River bridges.

This is actually the simplest part of the book. We wholeheartedly acknowledge Cheryl Towers and Harold Maguire, our intrepid publishers, who conceived of this idea, suggested the book and spurred us onward.

We would also like to acknowledge the support of the various entities that own and maintain the bridges within the city. In our previous outing when we explored Pittsburgh's city steps, we had unprecedented cooperation and support from various officials within the city government. In this project we discovered the same generous and cooperative attitude from not only the city but also Allegheny County, PennDOT and the Port Authority of Allegheny County. All members of these organizations have been thoroughly supportive and generous in the sharing of information, data, and perhaps most importantly, their time.

Mark Stem, City of Pittsburgh Department of Public Works, Bureau of Engineering and Construction, aided us significantly in sharing his knowledge and providing us access to that department's wealth of information. Thanks also to Mark and to Jim Dwyer of the Port Authority for providing critical reviews of the manuscript. However, Bob Regan takes full credit for any remaining errors.

Bob Regan and Tim Fabian

Opposite page: *A view of the Point. The Fort Duquesne Bridge is to the left and the Fort Pitt Bridge is on the right.*

P R E F A C E

I still vividly recall a Calvin and Hobbes comic strip that I read long before moving to Pittsburgh. In the strip Calvin, a precocious child, and his stuffed tiger (who comes alive in Calvin's imagination) are viewed lying on a hillside looking up at the sky.

> Calvin: "Where do you suppose we go when we die?"
> Hobbes: "Pittsburgh?"
> Then a pause.
> Calvin: "If we're good or if we're bad?"

Certainly, years ago, the answer to this metaphysical question would have been "If we're bad." Indeed Pittsburgh once led the nation in air and water pollution as well as industrial accidents and disease. In the

1940s, when asked how to best improve conditions in Pittsburgh, Frank Lloyd Wright responded that "It'd be cheaper to abandon it."

Fortunately no one followed his advice, and now everyone is becoming more and more aware of the many charming aspects of this city that were hidden beneath a blanket of smoke and soot for so long. So much so that Pittsburgh is now considered one of the best places to live in America, as confirmed by Rand McNally's *Places Rated Almanac* in 1985. In the May 18, 2003 weekend edition, *U.S. News* designated Pittsburgh as the second most beautiful place in America (second only to Sedona, Arizona). Specifically the magazine stated:

> *In a nation with a wealth of stunning cities full of compelling stories, ranking Pittsburgh as the No. 2 beauty spot is perhaps our most surprising choice. But the Steel City's aesthetic appeal is undeniable, as is its very American capacity for renewal. Standing atop Mount Washington, the steep hill that rises giddily on the city's south side, sightseers enjoy the unforgettable panorama of the Allegheny and Monongahela rivers flowing together to create the mighty Ohio. . . we salute its reinvention into one of America's most scenic and livable communities.*

Indeed, the 'burgh has a number of many unique features which native Pittsburghers should recognize and take great pride in. In a previous book (*The Steps of Pittsburgh: Portrait of a City*), we detailed one of these. This book offers a view of another set of features that are intimately connected with Pittsburgh, features that, in fact, distinguish it from all other cities *in the world*. Perhaps the books should be called a Pittsburgh Pride series. It is our hope that they contribute to helping ensure that the entire world realizes that the answer to Calvin's simple yet profound question is now a resounding "IF WE'RE GOOD!"

Bob Regan, 2006

INTRODUCTION

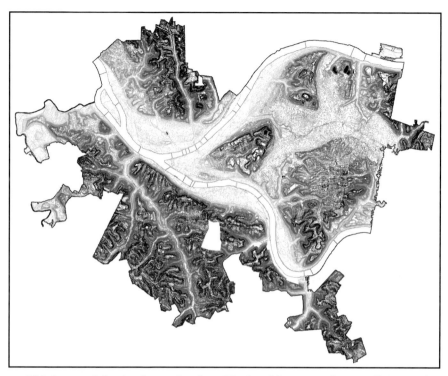

This image of the city dramatizes how Pittsburgh's topography contributes to the need for bridges (and tunnels and steps).

For good or bad topography has played a significant role in Pittsburgh's history and development. Even today, it has been estimated that 40% of the city is not suitable for building due to steep topography. The topography and the rivers have presented challenges to providing suitable means of access and transportation to all sections of the city. Vertical public mass transportation systems, i.e., city steps and inclines, helped Pittsburghers reach the many hillsides where the majority of them dwelt. Bridges, the horizontal equivalent of these vertical systems, helped ford the streams and rivers and cross over the many valleys. There are so many bridges in the city and surrounding area that we hardly notice them in our daily travels. Yet many are engineering marvels, each has a story, and most are visually appealing, both from afar and up close in their many intricate details.

(Note: Text continues on page 4.)

View of the Point *lithograph by T. M. Fowler, 1902, is from Mount Washington showing Point Bridge # 1 in the middle. The bridge over the*

Allegheny from the Point to what was then the City of Manchester is the Union Bridge (middle left). Courtesy of the Carnegie Library of Pittsburgh.

Indeed Pittsburgh has long been alluded to as "The City of Bridges." This is quite an appropriate sobriquet when you consider that every road into and out of the city has bridges. Pittsburgh has every type of conventional bridge except for a drawbridge. However, in keeping with the nature of the city, it also has many unconventional, unique bridges that add flavor to the city's spans. Some of these are the underground bridge, the recycled bridge, the two-in-one bridge, the fake bridge, the bridge inside a building, a landmark bridge guarded by panthers, and, nearby, a bridge whose name is subject to change every year.

Pittsburgh bridges also span almost the entire spectrum of bridge building styles going back to ancient Roman stone arch bridges. This city of bridges has contributed significantly to the development of bridge building technology from John Roebling's wire rope or cable to the Fort Pitt Bridge which was the first in the world built using computer-aided design.

This book is a celebration of the area's bridges; it is not a detailed engineering study nor an enumeration of every bridge to be found locally. Fortunately, those have been done in both print and electronic media. The late Walter Kidney's book, *Pittsburgh Bridges, Architecture and Engineering*, published by Pittsburgh History and Landmarks Foundation, is a detailed study of the bridges. The Web site www.pgh-bridges.com offers a detailed inventory, catalog, and pictorial survey of all the bridges.

This book serves as a complement to these excellent resources for all, and as an introduction to these resources for many. Our approach is rather a more personal story of the bridges, a bridge overview from a Pittsburgher's point of view, if you will. Another benefit from such an excursion is learning more about bridges in general which will make future trips more enjoyable as you appreciate the bridges you encounter and undoubtedly compare them to those back home in the 'burgh.

So please join us as we examine these proud silent-serving structures that are such an integral part of the city's fabric of life.

> Author's Note: The first time a bridge is mentioned in the text we provide both official and vernacular names but often defer to the familiar when discussing the bridge.

Opposite page: *The West End Bridge over the Ohio River is owned by PennDOT and was constructed in 1932.*

PART I
BRIDGE BACKGROUND

View of the P. J. McArdle Roadway Viaduct #2 (1935).

Bridge Basics

Before we delve into the city's bridges let's first explore some bridge basics, namely the definition of the word, the types of bridges, and their history.

What is a bridge?

The basic definition of a bridge taken from the *Oxford English Dictionary* is "a structure that allows people or vehicles to cross an obstacle, such as a river, canal, railway, etc."

The word derives from an old Norse word, *brygga*, meaning log, beam, and hence, wooden causeway. Additional meanings have been attached to the basic definition since 1450 when it was extended to include the hard ridge that forms the upper part of the nose. In 1607 the definition was extended still further to include the wooden support that holds the strings up in a violin. Additional definitions, familiar to us all include a denture anchored to teeth on either side of missing teeth; the upper deck of a ship where the captain pilots; a type of loan; and many electronic computer references.

One definition that is noticeably absent is that of the card game for four players based on whist. Although the game has been called "bridge" since the mid-nineteenth century, it has a different word origin. The term has been traced back to the Russian *birich* meaning a call and also to Turkish *bir-uc* meaning one-three, since one hand is exposed and three are concealed.

But for our purposes we will abide by the oldest and original meaning of the word, a structure built to span a gorge, valley, road, railroad track, river or any other physical obstacle. Typically a bridge is used for train, pedestrian or road traffic or may carry a pipeline or water. A bridge that has a series of spans, typically arches, is called a *viaduct* (and Pittsburgh has several). An *aqueduct* (Pittsburgh has had two) is a bridge carrying water.

Pittsburgh's Aqueducts and Viaducts		
	Name	Date
Aqueducts	Allegheny Canal (a/k/a Pennsylvania Canal)	1829 (original); 1845 (replacement)
Viaducts	Brilliant Cutoff	1903
	P. J. McArdle Roadway Viaduct No. 1	1935
	P. J. McArdle Roadway Viaduct No. 2	1935
	Lincoln Avenue Viaduct	1906

BRIDGE TYPES

Basically there are only three types of bridges. However, no area of engineering or science can survive with such a simple arrangement and thus many variations on these three basic themes have evolved.

The three basic types of bridges are *beam, arch* and *suspension*. The most significant difference between the three is the distance they can cross between supports, called the *bridge span*. A *simple beam* bridge can typically span 200 feet, a *basic arch* bridge up to 800 feet and a *suspension* bridge up to 10,000 feet.

A *beam* bridge is a horizontal beam supported at each end by piers. The farther apart the piers are spaced, the larger the beam must become, thus the limitation on the length of an effective beam bridge span. Beam bridges are easy to build, inexpensive relative to other bridge types and widely used in urban and rural settings.

A good example of a beam bridge is the Veterans Bridge carrying I-579 over the Allegheny River (see page 33).

The *arch* bridge is a curved structure with supports on both ends; it has been used for centuries throughout the world. A simple arch bridge reaches across a span in an arching shape rather than straight across as the beam bridge does. When considering the sturdiness of the arch it is interesting to recall da Vinci's comment that, "An arch consists of two weaknesses, which, leaning on each other become a strength."

Arch bridges are popular as a wide range of material can be used for their construction. However, they are relatively expensive to construct.

The Lincoln Avenue Viaduct at the top of the photo straddles Washington Boulevard. The Brilliant Cutoff Viaduct (railroad) is seen in the background.

Examples of arch bridges in Pittsburgh include the 40th Street Bridge (page 72-73) and the spectacular stone arch railroad bridge off Washington Boulevard near the Lincoln Avenue Bridge (above), itself also an arch bridge.

A *suspension* bridge, as the name indicates, has its deck suspended from cables and towers. Although these bridges can span great distances, they are quite expensive in terms of material and time to build. The only true (i.e. externally anchored) suspension bridge in the city of Pittsburgh is the South 10th Street Bridge spanning the Monongahela River (page 41). However, examples of what are termed *self-anchored suspension* bridges include the Roberto Clemente (6th Street), Andy

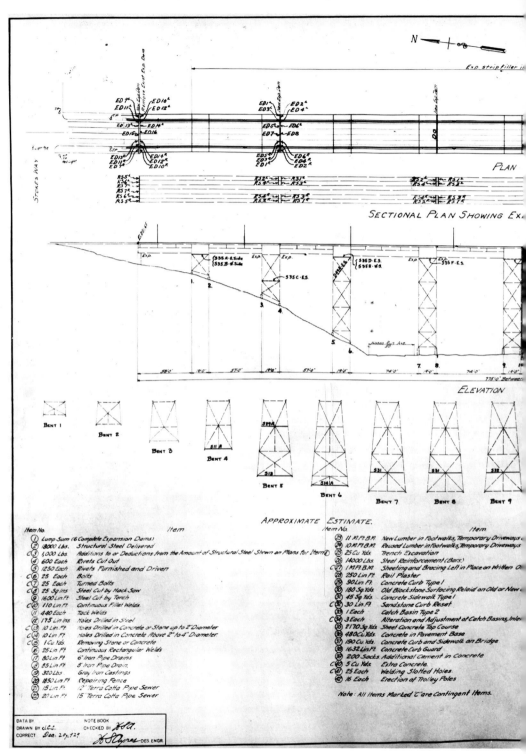

Drawing, Shadeland Avenue Bridge over Woods Run.
General plan and elevations. 1928/1929.

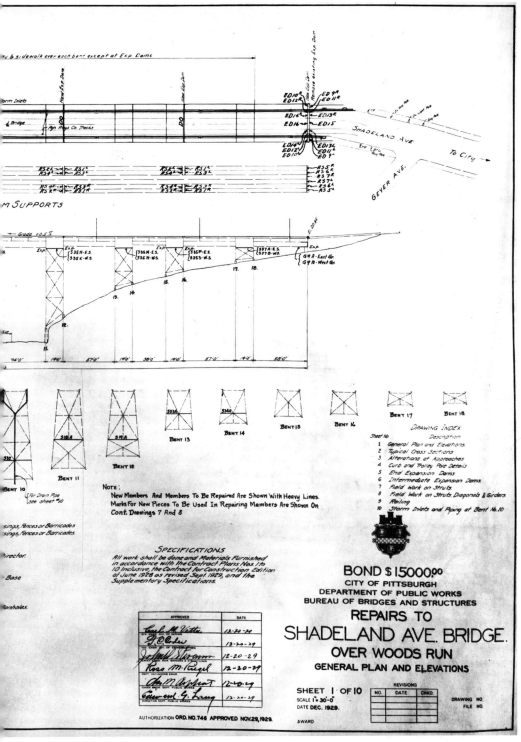

Courtesy of City of Pittsburgh Department of Public Works, Bureau of Engineering and Construction.

Warhol (7th Street), and Rachel Carson (9th Street) Bridges over the Allegheny River (page 68). They were the first of this type built in the United States. ("Self-anchored" means that the ends of the cables are connected to the bridge deck rather than anchored in massive concrete anchorages as is the case of a true suspension bridge.)

Some variations on the basic themes include the *truss* bridge, *cable-stayed* bridge and the *cantilever* bridge. The truss bridge could be considered a variation on the basic beam bridge as it allows for a longer span. It is a simple skeletal structure consisting of lattices formed of straight members in a triangular pattern. The patterns vary and various types of truss designs are named for the engineers who created them, e.g., the Glenwood Bridge can be described as having a *Warren* Truss (page 14). The truss construction is what George Ferris used in the development of his rotating wheel for the 1893 World's Fair that was an answer to the Eiffel Tower developed for the 1889 Fair in Paris (page 29). A covered bridge doesn't appear to be a truss bridge, but it is.

Cable-stayed bridges were developed in the 1950s and resemble suspension bridges, except that the deck is supported by cables attached to one or more towers on the bridges. This is one of the most spectacular

View of Monongahela River bridges looking northwest. The Panhandle (light rail) Bridge is in the foreground followed by the Smithfield Street, Fort Pitt and West End bridges.

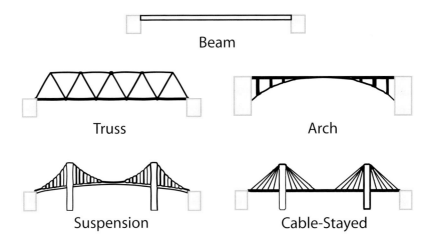

Beam

Truss

Arch

Suspension

Cable-Stayed

types of bridge. There are none in Pittsburgh, but the nearby Veterans Memorial Bridge across the Ohio River connecting Weirton, West Virginia with Steubenville, Ohio is worth a 40-minute drive for bridge aficionados. This one was designed by Pittsburgh's Michael Baker, Jr., Inc. in 1978 and opened in 1990 (page 15).

Not all bridges that have an arch shape are arch bridges; many are a variation called a *cantilever*. To the layman the difference is difficult to discern (and may not be important) except if one witnesses the bridge during the construction phase. As Joseph White noted in his 1928 book on Pittsburgh bridges:

> *A cantilever bridge projects over midstream and is so balanced that the projected part or bracket is counter-weighted and anchored down by the shore ends of the structure. In a cantilever the stability of the structure depends upon shore anchorage, whereas the stability of the arch depends upon the locking member over midstream. In a cantilever bridge, construction proceeds from the shore with no temporary supports over the river channel, whereas an arch during construction is usually supported. . . until the locking member at the center is placed. Because it is not necessary to block a river channel during construction. . . cantilever bridges are extensively used.*

The Liberty Bridge (pages 18 and 65) connecting downtown to the Liberty Tunnels on the South Side is a cantilever bridge as described by White. However, such bridges are not limited to crossing rivers as the East Street (E. H. Swindell) Bridge over I-279 attests (page 17).

White also notes that,

> *. . . a simple way to recognize a cantilever bridge is to stand at a point where the entire structure can be viewed; if the general proportions of the bridge conveys the impression that the structure would remain standing if a section in the center were removed, it is probably a cantilever bridge. On the other hand, if it is apparent that the entire span would collapse if cut at the center, it is not a cantilever.*

The general appearance of a bridge can also lead to a description of the bridge as a *deck bridge* or a *through bridge*. In a deck bridge, all the bridge structure is beneath the roadway or deck and the deck is open to the sky. Conversely in a through bridge, the deck traverses through the structural fabric of the bridge. One only need to travel over the Liberty and Smithfield Street (page 28) bridges to notice the difference.

Interestingly, Pittsburgh has been almost completely self-sustaining as a source of bridge material. In the early days there was a bounty of trees that provided the lumber for wooden bridges. With the advent of steel in bridge building, the only missing ingredient was iron ore that was routinely transported from Minnesota.

The Glenwood Bridge over the Monongahela River utilizes Warren Truss construction.

The Veterans Memorial Bridge is a magnificent example of cable-stay construction and was designed in 1978 by the Pittsburgh firm of Michael Baker, Jr., Inc. It carries Route 22 over the Ohio River between Weirton, West Virginia and Steubenville, Ohio. The bridge opened in 1990.

A Brief Bridge Vocabulary	
Abutment	A support for the end of a bridge.
Anchorage	A foundation structure that secures suspension bridge cables.
Aqueduct	An elevated structure carrying water.
Arch	A semicircular structure.
Beam	A rigid, horizontal structural element that supports vertical loads by resisting bending.
Beam bridge	A bridge with a horizontal beam supported by vertical piers.
Cable	A large-diameter steel rope made of many smaller steel strands. Suspenders, also called hangers, are attached along its length to support the deck.
Caisson	Cylindrical concrete foundation that penetrates through 'unsuitable soil' to rest on good soil or bedrock. Also, a watertight, dry chamber that permits excavation and other work to be performed underwater.

A BRIEF BRIDGE VOCABULARY	
Cantilever	Structural member that projects beyond a supporting column or wall and is counterbalanced or supported only at one end, like a shelf bracket or diving board.
Catenary	The curve formed by a cable hanging freely between two supports. The curved cables of a suspension bridge are also called catenaries.
Concrete	An artificial, stone like building material made by combining cement with aggregate and water.
Dead load	The weight of all the parts of the bridge.
Expansion joint	A meeting between two parts of a structure that is designed to accommodate movement due to heat, moisture and ground motions while protecting the structure from damage.
Girder	A horizontal structure member that supports vertical loads. A girder is larger than a beam and can be made of multiple plates of steel or other material.
Live load	The weight of anything that is not part of the bridge.
Pier	A vertical bridge support.
Pylon	Tower from which cables radiate in a cable-stayed bridge.

This bridge carries Ridge Avenue over a set of railroad tracks near West Park on the North Side. Note the truss construction to the left of the pedestrians.

A BRIEF BRIDGE VOCABULARY	
Reinforced concrete	Concrete that has been reinforced with embedded steel rods or mesh.
Roadway	The part of a bridge that carries vehicles, also called the deck.
Span	The horizontal distance between two bridge supports.
Substructure	The portion of a bridge structure including abutments and piers that support the substructure.
Superstructure	The portion of a bridge that carries the traffic load and passes that load onto the substructure.
Suspenders	Cables of a suspension bridge that hang from the main cable to support the deck. Also called hangers.
Tower	The vertical element in suspension bridges from which cables are hung.
Trestle	A horizontal beam or bar held up by two pair of divergent legs and used as a support.
Truss	A rigid structure that is made up of interlocking triangles.
Viaduct	An elevated roadway. More precisely, a series of spans or arches used to carry a road or railroad over terrain or other roadways.

The E. H. Swindell Bridge over I-279 is an example of cantilever bridge construction.

Liberty Bridge photo taken from the top of the Liberty Tubes, April 1933. The Monongahela Railroad (Panhandle) Bridge is to the left of the Liberty Bridge; the Smithfield Street Bridge is to the far left. Courtesy of City of Pittsburgh Department of Public Works, Bureau of Engineering and Construction.

Bridge History

The Pont-du-Gard aqueduct in France was constructed by the Romans in the process of expanding their empire. Photo by Holly Van Dine.

Our fascination with bridges is undoubtedly deeply rooted in our genetic makeup. Perhaps during the early development of our species, a tree fell across a river or valley and all of a sudden a new area was opened to our prehistoric ancestors.

Indeed, the earliest bridges were simple logs or planks deliberately laid across streams or valleys (basic beam bridges). The Romans perfected the technique of building arch bridges in their construction of heavy masonry bridges throughout the Roman Empire. In their bridges large stone blocks were wedged against each other to form an arch. The central stone at the top of the arch was called the *keystone*. This term

NO 1. UNION PASSENGER P.R.R.
  " 2. BERMINGHAM STATION PANHANDLE R.R.
  " 3. P & L E. R.R. --------STATION
  " 4. B.& O. " ------- "
  " 5. P & W & B.R.& P.R.R.-- "
  " 6. POST OFFICE.
  " 7. EXPOSITION BUILDINGS.
  " 8. FORT PITT BLOCKHOUSE

PITTS

PENNS

19

DRAWN BY T.M.FOWLER MORRISVILLE PA.   COPYRIGHT BY

Pittsburgh map 1902. GPC Maps. Courtesy of the Library and Archives Division,
Historical Society of Western Pennsylvania, Pittsburgh, PA.

MON·ON·GA·HE·LA   RIVER.

RIVER

B. JAMES B MOYER

PUBLISHED BY T.M FOWLER & JAMES B MOYER.

BURGH,

IA.

NO 9. COURT HOUSE
" 10. FARMERS SAVINGS BANK.
" 12. ARROTT BUILDING.
" 13. PEOPLES SAVINGS BANK
" 14. FRICK   BUILDING
" 15. CARNEGIE   ------ "
" 16. PARK   ------ "

should be familiar to all residents of the Keystone State, so called as Pennsylvania served as the "keystone" for the six original states to the north and the six to the south during the early post-colonial era.

The Roman bridges were not simple single arch bridges but rather often an array of arches and even multi-tiered arches. In addition to the basic building stones, the Romans also used concrete.

The Romans were prolific bridge builders, but not much changed in the design and construction of bridges until the 12th century.

At that time the Holy Roman Empire's Catholic priests and professionals took over bridge building as they realized that bridges helped communication vital to developing society.

In France a new order of priests, the *Freres du Pont*, was established to design and build bridges. Not surprisingly, many of the bridges were adorned with statues of saints and contained small chapels. (In keeping with contemporary values, many of today's bridges do not contain small rooms dedicated to prayer but rather to the collection of tolls.)

However, for over 500 years the bridges designed and built by the Catholic priests with a penchant for engineering changed very little. During this time the technology for concrete was lost and most bridges were built with brick and mortar. It was not until the eighteenth century when French army engineers took over bridge building that bridge professionals became involved in the design and construction of bridges.

The introduction of bridge professionals, the widespread use of iron in the 18th century, and the rapid expansion of railroads during the 19th century spurred much development in bridge technology. Another contributing factor was the number of disasters and deaths in the failure of many early railroad bridges. During the first part of the nineteenth century, iron was the bridge building material of choice. Truss design was also developed to provide additional strength to the basic bridge designs required for the heavier loads of trains.

Steel was developed in the mid-19th century and soon introduced into bridge building. By the end of the century steel had replaced all other materials as the prime material for bridge building. In addition, many bridges were built using the ideas of Gustav Eiffel as exemplified in the tower he built for the 1889 World's Fair. It is interesting to note that two well known engineering constructs, the Eiffel Tower and the Ferris Wheel, are based on bridge technology—or vice versa.

Suspension bridges developed during this period were initially built using iron but really came into their own due to John A. Roebling, the father of modern suspension bridge design. He pioneered the use of steel in suspension bridges and developed the technology to make wire cables. Truly, there was more development in bridge building, design, technology and material during the 19th century than in the preceding 2,000-3,000 years.

Major developments in bridge design and material since Roebling's time include the cable-stayed bridge in the mid-20th century and the reintroduction of concrete as a building material. Once rediscovered, it was improved for bridge construction with the development of the technology to reinforce it with re-bar. Now concrete is as important to bridge building as steel ever was.

Of course wood has also been used throughout the entire history of bridge building, and thankfully, many wooden covered bridges still remain throughout the country.

Detail of arch from the Larimer Avenue Bridge.

Above: *Detail of wire cable used in suspension bridges. The original technology was developed by John A. Roebling.* Below: *Detail of the steel eyebar chain on the Rachel Carson Bridge.*

Pittsburgh's Bridge Pioneers

Pittsburgh's need for bridges all but guaranteed that it would also become a mecca for innovation and technology. Three fathers of modern bridge design—Roebling, Lindenthal and Ferris—all have roots here. In addition, George Richardson presided over the city's most prolific era of bridge building. And as if that weren't enough, the city's bridge building expertise is felt far and wide (see Beyond Pittsburgh beginning on page 44), due in no small part to these pioneers.

John A. Roebling portrait. Courtesy Carnegie Library of Pittsburgh.

Former Sixth Street Bridge designed by John A. Roebling opened in 1846 and was abandoned in 1892. Courtesy of Carnegie Library.

John Augustus Roebling: (1806-1869) was born in Muhlhausen, Germany and became interested in suspension bridges while studying at the University of Berlin and the Polytechnic Institute of Berlin. Although an engineer, he was also deeply involved in addressing social problems of the time. Eventually, he, his younger brother and a group of other young people emigrated to the United States to seek political and religious freedom, and set up an ideal community. Although headed for the western United States, with resources dwindling they settled near Pittsburgh and originally called their settlement Germania, later to become known as Saxonburg.

Once the settlement was established Roebling gained employment with the Commonwealth of Pennsylvania as an engineer on the Pennsylvania Canal. This employment led to his development of America's first wire rope. Surprisingly, he did not develop the rope for bridges, but rather for the canal's portage railways, which carried the canal barges up the side of the mountains. These railways used large (9 inch diameter) hemp ropes, which were unwieldy and broke often.

With guidance from an obscure German technical engineering paper, Roebling decided to try and fabricate a rope made of wire, which he accomplished in 1840. Although he initially met resistance, the state finally accepted the design a year later, and the 1-1/4 inch diameter wire rope successfully replaced the old hemp rope.

Shortly afterward he adopted wire rope to his true love, suspension bridges, and did so for the first time with the Allegheny Aqueduct Bridge (1845) for the Pennsylvania Canal over the Allegheny River in Pittsburgh. Following the design of this bridge he then designed the Smithfield Street Bridge (1846) and the Niagara Gorge Bridge (1850), which brought him worldwide fame.

As his fame and business increased, Roebling established a wire rope factory in Trenton, New Jersey, and in 1849 moved from Saxonburg. He died in 1869 during his construction of the Brooklyn Bridge, leaving his son, Washington, to finish it. Although his wire rope invention is often connected to bridges it was also used in elevators, anti-submarine netting, and in aircraft controls, most notably in Charles Lindbergh's *Spirit of St. Louis.*

Gustav Lindenthal portrait. Courtesy of Bob Singleton, the Greater Astoria Historical Society.

The present-day Smithfield Street Bridge is a lenticular truss, through bridge design by Gustav Lindenthal. It opened in 1883 and was widened in 1892.

Gustav Lindenthal: (1850-1935), designer of today's Smithfield Street Bridge, had several things in common with two other noted Pittsburgh bridge engineers, John Roebling and George Ferris. Like Roebling, he emigrated from a German speaking country, Austria, and had attended a polytechnic school in his native country. He first started working with railroads, which led him to designing bridges, as was the case with George Ferris. Lindenthal came to the United States in 1874 and gained employment as an engineer for the Centennial Exposition in Philadelphia. He moved to Pittsburgh in 1877, and ultimately started his own engineering practice. By the turn of the century, he was well known and respected throughout the engineering community, due in large part to his work on the Smithfield Street Bridge. His reputation led him to be selected as Commissioner of Bridges in New York City in 1902. After many successful years in the United States, he returned to his native land where he taught at several technical universities until his death in 1935.

George W. G. Ferris: (1859-1896) Illinois born civil engineer George W. G. Ferris gave the world the Ferris Wheel and as is too often the case, suffered for it. A graduate of Rensselaer Polytechnic Institute, he began his career in the railroad industry and through that became interested in bridge building and ultimately started designing bridges and trestles. Understanding the role that bridges would play in this developing country and concerned for bridge safety, he moved to the City of Bridges and founded G. W. G. Ferris & Co., a firm that tested and inspected metals for bridges.

With the advent of the Chicago World's Fair of 1893 there was a desire to build an engineering marvel that would outshine the Eiffel Tower built for the 1889 Paris exhibition. At a Saturday afternoon lunch, Ferris came up with the idea of his wheel sketching out all the details (which never varied) on several napkins. Despite the ridicule of other

Left: *The Ferris Wheel utilizes truss construction typical in many bridge designs. Courtesy of the Paul V. Galvin Library, Illinois Institute of Technology.* Right: *George W. G. Ferris. Courtesy of Carnegie Library of Pittsburgh.*

engineers and the hesitancy of the World's Fair director, he persevered, finally winning approval only 22 weeks before the opening of the fair. However, he had to fund the project himself. (In contrast, Eiffel had two years and full government funding to build his tower.)

Despite the many obstacles including the notorious Chicago winter weather, Ferris completed the wheel only seven weeks behind schedule and it soon became the high point of the Fair. The wheel was 250 feet high and carried 36 cars, each holding 40 passengers. It was absolutely stable even with the gusty Lake Michigan winds. Today, the Eye, the Millennium Wheel on the banks of the Thames River in London, offers riders an experience similar to that of Ferris's original wheel.

Ferris never profited from his invention and died a lonely, bankrupt, sickly and broken man, just 37 years old, on November 21, 1896 in Pittsburgh's Mercy Hospital.

George S. Richardson.
Courtesy of HDR Engineering, Inc.

George S. Richardson: (1896-1988) was a bridge designer and engineer with Allegheny County's Bureau of Bridges, the predecessor to today's Department of Public Works. He undoubtedly had a greater impact and influence in developing many of the city's most notable bridges than any other engineer. His period of tenure in the county's Bureau of Bridges marked an unprecedented era of bridge building. He and his

Known for years as the Homestead High Level Bridge but sporting a recent change of name to the Homestead Grays Bridge, this dramatic span (a deck truss bridge) connects the Squirrel Hill neighborhood of Pittsburgh to the Borough of Homestead on the south shore of the Monongahela River. The new name honors the Homestead Grays, a national power in the old Negro Baseball League.

staff were responsible for the Three Sisters bridges (Roberto Clemente, Andy Warhol, and Rachel Carson bridges over the Allegheny River); the West End Bridge over the Ohio River; plus the South 10th Street and the Homestead Grays bridges over the Monongahela, among others. After his county service, he was involved in the founding of a local engineering firm, Richardson, Gordon, and Associates (RGA), that was purchased in 1985 by HDR Engineering, which is still in existence today.

PART II

THE CITY OF BRIDGES

This view of seven downtown bridges crossing the Allegheny River demonstrates the incredible variety of Pittsburgh bridge styles. From top to bottom they are the 16th Street (trussed through arch), the Veterans (beam), Fort Wayne Railroad (double Warren truss), the Three Sisters (self-anchored suspension) and Fort Duquesne (arch with truss-braced deck).

THE HEAD COUNT

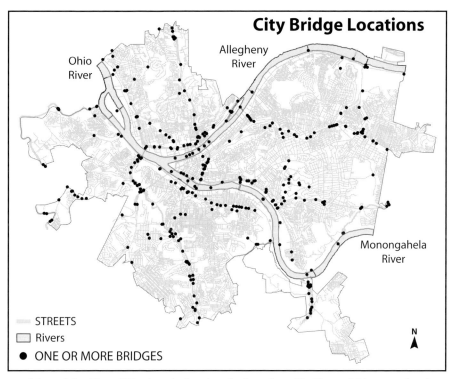

City Bridge Locations

Ohio River

Allegheny River

Monongahela River

STREETS
Rivers
● ONE OR MORE BRIDGES

N

Map of the City of Pittsburgh showing the location of bridges within or at the city boundaries. Several of the bullets are the location of more than one bridge.

Jerry DiPaola, writing in the *Pittsburgh Tribune-Review* on May 9, 2004 noted that, "The first thing new Steelers running back Duce Staley noticed about his new home were all the bridges crossing Pittsburgh's three rivers. 'There are over 40-50 bridges,' Staley said. 'C'mon.'"

Duce didn't know the half of it. In fact there are *many* more than fifty bridges and Pittsburgh is routinely alluded to as the City of Bridges. Some claim that only one other city in the world—Venice, Italy—has more bridges. The Venice Bureau of Tourism states that the city has "almost 400" bridges in total, and further, Venice has 120 islands and 177 canals with most of the bridges merely small footbridges.

If Pittsburgh is to validly lay claim to the title City of Bridges, it is important to document the number of bridges there are in the city. Unfortunately, there have been many conflicting estimates of this number. A great deal of the confusion is due to the fact that many estimates, although stated for Pittsburgh, are actually for Allegheny County and/or the greater Pittsburgh Metropolitan Area.

The various estimates depend also on the definition of a bridge. The National Bridge Inspection Standard (NBIS) definition is that of a structure of length 20 feet or greater. The definition of the length of a bridge can be confusing as the length of the Fort Pitt Bridge includes the length of the Fort Pitt Tunnel. Another factor is the various owners of the bridges within the city, a factor not static as bridge ownerships are often transferred between government entities.

Owners of bridges include the City of Pittsburgh, Allegheny County, Pennsylvania Department of Transportation (PennDOT), Port Authority of Allegheny County (Port Authority) and the various railroads that traverse the city. Two rules of ownership: Allegheny County typically owns all the non-interstate highway bridges that span the city limits, e.g. connecting the city with another municipality. To make matters a bit more complicated, ownership of a bridge crossing a railroad is split between the owner of the railroad and the owner of the road, according to the Public Utilities Commission.

CITY OF PITTSBURGH

The current City of Pittsburgh bridge database indicates that the city owns 123 bridges. This includes four tunnels (Corliss Tunnel, the approach to the Bloomfield Bridge and two pedestrian tunnels) and

The top of the West End Bridge is visible at the bottom of the photo. The Ohio River Connecting Railroad Bridge is in the middle with the McKees Rocks Bridge in the background.

three bridges that are jointly owned with the Port Authority or PennDOT and reported in their data. The city's database does *not* include the six bridges along the Eliza Furnace Trail and the new South 10th and 15th Street footbridges. Also not included are the Hot Metal and Mon Connecting Railroad Bridges that are in the process of transference from the Urban Redevelopment Authority (URA) to the city. In short, removing the seven tunnels and jointly owned bridges plus adding these ten other bridges yields a total of 126 bridges owned by the city.

ALLEGHENY COUNTY

Allegheny County sports a total of 522 bridges within the county limits. Analysis of their database, inspection of maps and discussions with county public works personnel revealed that only 21 of these 522 are within the city limits or at the boundary.

PENNDOT

Data extracted from PennDOT's Bridge Management System for structures greater than eight feet located within the city show 204 such structures. The key word here is *structures* as it includes bridge ramps, cliff supports and tunnels. Inspection of their data also raises the question as to what constitutes a bridge. For example, does an interstate

The Fort Duquesne Bridge (foreground) underwent repainting in 2004-2005 which is the reason for the drapery. The Fort Pitt Bridge is in the background.

The Charles Street Bridge spans I-279.

ramp qualify, or do the elevated sections of roadways, typified by those around Heinz Field? Jim Dwyer of the Port Authority who is a bridge engineer with decades of experience says, "if it has supports, abutments, and spans, it is a bridge." In the case of elevated roadways, some architects have a difference of opinion, but we will adhere to the bridge engineers' definition. (Think of it this way: if all elevated roadways were considered bridges, Los Angeles would have more bridges than any other city.)

Using this definition, a detailed inspection of the PennDOT data would disqualify 18 of their structures, resulting in 186 bridges owned by them within the city.

Port Authority

The Port Authority of Allegheny County has a total of 80 bridges, 42 of which are within the city limits; five are pedestrian bridges.

Railroad Companies

It is difficult to obtain information from the railroads about their bridges. However, the city's Geographic Information System (GIS) digital spatial database contains detailed maps of active and unused rail lines in the city and a listing of rail structures. Using this information in concert with inspection of detailed aerial photos and a physical survey on the ground, we have counted 71 railroad bridges within or at the city limits.

SUMMARY OF THE COUNT

In our survey we included all bridges (not just those greater than 20 feet), as the tabulations from foreign countries certainly don't abide by NBIS definitions, and we considered *only* the bridges within the City of Pittsburgh or at the city limits.

In 2001, Malcolm Lindsay generously developed a database of the bridges within the entire area for the Carnegie Library of Pittsburgh. That database reveals 380 bridges in the City of Pittsburgh. However within that segment of the database, there are 11 tunnels, duplicates, and private pedestrian bridges. Also, 15 of the previously excluded PennDOT structures were included in the database. Removing all of these would leave 354 bridges in the city.

Comparison of Lindsay's database with those previously noted revealed that there were 39 bridges *not* listed in this database. In addition this database contains reference to only 22 railroad bridges. Consequently, adding the 39 bridges to this data plus an additional 49 railroad bridges (difference between our noted 71 railroad bridges and the 22 reported) yields 442 bridges. Again we must add those not reported in any database, i.e., the new South 10th and 15th Street footbridges and the Hot Metal and Mon Connecting Bridges, bringing the total to 446 bridges in the City of Pittsburgh.

OTHER ANALYSES USING GIS

The city's Geographic Information System (GIS) digital database includes detailed mappings of all the streets in the city. Various components include bridges, some city-owned, some not, for a total of 123 structures. However, four are tunnels; these were removed from the data and ten additional bridges (six along the Eliza Furnace bicycle trail; the new 10th and 15th Street pedestrian bridges; the Hot Metal and Mon Connecting Bridges) were added.

This information was then visually examined to develop a new layer of data showing all the non-railroad bridges within or at the city limits. This yielded 223 bridges. It is interesting to note that a map of all these bridges shows that, with the exception of the I-279 corridor, the bridge pattern was quite similar to that of the rail lines.

The Smithfield Street Bridge won designation by the Association for Bridge Construction and Design in 1995 as the outstanding rehabilitative bridge.

With the addition of the 71 railroad bridges, the total number obtained in this manner would be 294 bridges. However, this is only the number that would be observable from aerial photography (the basis for the mapping). Subtle and small bridges would not be detected and complex structures could not be resolved. Thus this estimate is extremely conservative.

THE FINAL TALLY

The two independent compilations of bridge data show that there are well over 400 bridges within the City of Pittsburgh. Such an estimate is also supported by the analysis of aerial survey mapping data showing almost 300 major structures.

Thus the best estimate of the number of bridges within the City of Pittsburgh is 446. The area of the city is 58.24 square miles. This means that there are 7.6 bridges per square mile. Anyway you look at it, Pittsburgh can validly claim the title of "City of Bridges", a title no longer carrying the disclaimer that it is second only to Venice, Italy with its approximately 400 (small) bridges.

The South 10th Street Bridge (1931) is the only true suspension bridge in the City of Pittsburgh.

Some may say that Saint Petersburg, Russia, known as "The Venice of the North", has more bridges than Pittsburgh. However, while the abundance of islands in that fair city led to the construction of a multitude of bridges, there are only 308 within the city limits. The number of bridges exceeds Pittsburgh's if and only if those in the suburbs of St. Petersburg are counted, as then there are 534, a number that has sometimes been reported for the city itself. But if that is the case, Pittsburgh can count its suburbs, too, and would once again surge into the lead.

Number of Pittsburgh Bridges	
Owned and Maintained by	Bridges
Allegheny County	21
City of Pittsburgh	126
PennDOT	186
Port Authority	42
Railroads	71
Total	**446**

PENNSYLVANIA'S BRIDGES

As of December 2004, there were 594,470 bridges in the United States, according to *Better Roads* magazine. While Pennsylvania with 23,464 ranks eighth, southwestern Pennsylvania has more bridges per capita and per square mile than any other region in the United States, again according to *Better Roads*.

There are so many bridges in the Commonwealth of Pennsylvania that the Pennsylvania Department of Transportation is selling some. In an effort to preserve some of the state's historic bridges that need to be replaced due to load and width restrictions, PennDOT is marketing them to other agencies, nonprofit organizations and educational institutions for a nominal fee. It's a very positive program as the Federal Highway Administration will reimburse PennDOT up to 80% of the costs of dismantling the bridge to move it to its new home.

The Fort Pitt Bridge from the mouth of the Fort Pitt Tunnel facing downtown.

Beyond Numbers

33rd Street Railroad Bridge.

Numbers alone don't account for the title of City of Bridges. Equally important is the variety. Pittsburgh has or has had pedestrian, automobile, railroad, bus, light rail, water, hot metal, and incline-carrying bridges. It also has or has had covered bridges, wooden bridges, all steel bridges, toll bridges and bridges of every style, shape and form except for a drawbridge.

Many of the city's bridges are also downright beautiful. Indeed E. T. Heberston devoted an entire book to this topic in 1970 and notes that the "art qualities are ensured in Pittsburgh (bridges) by the collaboration of architects and engineers and by the function exercised by the Art Commission." The Art Commission, established in 1911, evaluates the form and appearance of all bridges costing more than $25,000. Their

The graceful Portal Bridge in Point State Park is unusual in that it supports an interstate highway (I-279).

approval is necessary prior to any bridge construction or reconstruction. One only need examine the Portal Bridge leading to Point State Park. Far from being strictly utilitarian, it is a work of art and quite striking when one considers that it supports an interstate highway.

In addition, PennDOT routinely seeks the advice of organizations such as the Downtown Partnership and the River Life Task Force on such matters as bridge color. It was this collaboration that led to the decision to paint all the major bridges in the downtown area yellow (actually, Aztec Gold) to reflect the Golden Triangle concept. As an aside, this color has a practical aspect in that it aids bridge inspection by highlighting stains and rust.

Because of the rich variety and number of bridges here, bridge engineers hold their annual International Bridge Conference in Pittsburgh. A highlight is a dinner cruise along the rivers in which the many bridges are visited. As the conference brochure states: "What better place to hold the International Bridge Conference than Pittsburgh, a city with 700 bridges, 15 spanning the downtown area alone." The conference is held in mid-June of each year as it has been for almost a quarter century. (*Author's note: the 700 is the IBC's estimate and includes bridges outside the city limits.*)

Beyond Pittsburgh

The bridge engineers come to Pittsburgh because the city is more than the "City of Bridges"—it is and has been a source of bridge expertise and technology recognized and used throughout the world. Also, as the "Steel City", Pittsburgh has provided material used to build bridges all over the world, in addition to construction material for other historic structures such as the Empire State Building and the Panama Canal.

The New River Gorge Bridge opened in 1977 and is located in the New River Gorge National River area of West Virginia. The bridge was designed by the Michael Baker Corporation and built by the American Bridge Corporation (formerly a division of U.S. Steel), both of Pittsburgh; it is owned and operated by the state of West Virginia. Photo courtesy of the National Park Service.

One example of the city's prowess in bridge technology used beyond our borders is the Eads Bridge over the Mississippi River (1874). This bridge was fabricated by the Keystone Bridge Company in Lawrenceville and then shipped to its present location; it was designed and built by James B. Eads.

This was the first bridge built exclusively using cantilever construction methods. With its three spans of more than 500 feet, it was called the greatest engineering feat of its kind. Unfortunately J. H. Linville, president of Keystone Bridge, said that the bridge design was "unsafe and impractical." The longevity of the bridge has since proven him wrong.

Another well-known bridge that resulted from the Pittsburgh area's wealth of bridge technology is the New River Gorge Bridge in Fayetteville, West Virginia. This bridge is 3,000 feet long with an arch spanning 1,700 feet. It was the longest steel arch bridge in the world until February, 2003 when the Lupu Bridge in Shanghai opened. The length of the West Virginia bridge and its spectacular setting and beauty are probably less responsible for its notoriety than the fact that it is closed one day a year to allow for bungee jumping, parachuting, rappelling and general pedestrian use. The bridge was designed by Pittsburgh's Michael Baker Company and built by the American Bridge Company of nearby Ambridge, Pennsylvania.

A Web site by Rich Koor (http://filebox.vt.edu/users/rkoors/Index. htm) offers vivid insights into the design and innovative construction of this bridge as well as links to tourism offices if you want to visit the area.

The James B. Eads Bridge opened in 1874 and spans the Mississippi River at Washington Street, St. Louis County, Missouri. It was fabricated by the Pittsburgh firm of Keystone Bridge Company, now part of the American Bridge Company, formerly a division of U.S. Steel. Photo by Paul Piaget, 1968. Library of Congress, Prints and Photographs Division, Historic American Buildings Survey, HABS,MO,96-SALU,77-1.

BRIDGE FIRSTS AND ACCOLADES

The Rachel Carson Bridge was the world's first
self-anchored suspension bridge. It opened in 1927.

Pittsburgh's place in bridge history is well established by virtue of noted bridge firsts along with prominent bridge engineers and bridge awards. Some of these are:

Bridge Firsts

- First all steel self-cleaning bridge—McFarren Avenue Bridge/ Duck Hollow
- First self-anchored suspension bridge—Rachel Carson
- First wire cable suspension bridge—Pennsylvania Canal
- First computer-aided designed bridge—Fort Pitt
- The oldest extant "lenticular truss style" bridge in the United States—Smithfield Street, 1883
- First and only three identical side-by-side bridges in the world— The Three Sisters (ironically, two of The Three Sisters are now named after men):

    Roberto Clemente

    Andy Warhol

    Rachel Carson

Noted Bridge Engineers

(see Bridge Pioneers profiles—page 25)
- John Roebling
- Gustav Lindenthal
- George Ferris
- George S. Richardson

Awards

- Panther Hollow Bridge—City Designated Landmark
- Schenley Park Bridge—City Designated Landmark
- 6th Street Bridge—most beautiful steel bridge of 1928—American Institute of Steel Construction
- Smithfield Street Bridge—Civil Engineering Historic Landmark, City Designated Landmark, and National Historic Landmark; outstanding rehabilitative bridge of 1995 by the Association for Bridge Construction and Design

BRIDGE SAFETY

PennDOT and its contractors conduct all official bridge inspections within the city. Here they inspect the 40th Street Bridge using a "snooper" truck.

Although we noted earlier that there are many positive reasons to live in Pittsburgh, it is not a desirable place to be if you suffer from *gephyrophobia*, or the fear of bridges. The word derives from the Greek words "gepyra" meaning bridge and "phobos" meaning fear.

Even if you are not fearful of bridges, you might express concern about the safety of bridges in an area that contains so many. A June 2003 report by the Washington-based Road Information Program stated that there are 1,210 bridges in the Pittsburgh urban area (another estimate!) and that 29% are classified as functionally obsolete, meaning that they no longer meet modern design standards for safety features such as lane width or alignment with connecting roads. The report also stated that all the bridges are safe although many have sustained significant deterioration to decks and major components.

However, one need not worry owing to the rigorous bridge inspection program mandated by the federal government and zealously followed or exceeded by all the owners of our bridges. Although the city and county used to do their own inspections, now all work is done by PennDOT (and their contractors) acting as the federal overseer for the bridges in the area. Normal procedure is for the bridges to undergo a rigorous inspection every two years. If there are some questions about the bridge as indicated by a load limit sign, then it is inspected annually. If any problems are noted the bridge may even be re-inspected every week or, in extreme cases, on a daily basis.

Bridge inspection is primarily visual, aided by non-destructive testing measurements such as ground penetrating radar, sonic techniques, and ultraviolet light.

Inspections are also sometimes ordered for bridges over the rivers that are susceptible to hits by barge tows. Should a collision occur, the barge captain must call the Coast Guard who alerts the bridge owner. Usually the bridge is immediately shut down and then inspected. During the floods of 2004, water affected the bridge supports on the Port Authority's light rail bridge across the Monongahela (the so-called Panhandle Bridge). This bridge was due for inspection in the near future, but the Port Authority did so immediately, even examining underwater, something usually done only every four years.

One should also keep in mind that the Pittsburgh area contains a large population of bridge engineers regularly traversing these structures and undoubtedly in doing so, scanning them. In addition the many professionals on the towboats traversing the rivers routinely examine the bridges and have noticed and reported problems in the past.

The next time you encounter a bridge inspection crew, usually recognizable by the "snooper truck" which permits inspection of the underneath of a bridge while parked on the deck, don't be annoyed by any traffic delay but rather be pleased that the safety of the bridge is being reassured.

BRIDGE DISASTERS

Although Pittsburgh area bridges are quite safe and there has been an absence of bridge problems in modern times, this was not always the case. Many of the early structures were wooden bridges that suffered a common fate—destruction by fire. That was the case in 1845 when the first bridge over the rivers, the original Smithfield Street Bridge, went up in flames.

The 16th Street Bridge had a checkered career. It was destroyed by fire in 1851 and rebuilt, but in 1865 two spans were washed away in a flood. Rebuilt once again, it was again destroyed by fire in 1918.

The original 30th Street Bridge built in 1887 was similarly destroyed by fire in 1921.

One of the most intriguing bridge fires, demonstrating the interaction of river traffic with the bridges, was the fate of the original 6th Street (St. Clair Street) Bridge. In the late 1880s, a sparrow's nest in the bridge was ignited by ash from a steamboat's smokestack and the bridge burned.

Another, more recent disaster occurred on October 19, 1903 when the Wabash Bridge, then under construction, collapsed killing ten workers. The last disaster, fortunately without fatalities, occurred in 1927 when the Mount Washington Roadway Bridge collapsed during construction.

Since that time there has not been a bridge collapse in the Commonwealth of Pennsylvania and there has *never* been a collapse of an operating bridge. However, this record was somewhat blemished in late 2005 with the collapse of a portion (one side girder) of a bridge over I-70 near Washington, PA.

The Greenfield Bridge (1923) carries Beechwood Boulevard across the Parkway East (I-376), and is overdue for repairs. The smaller bridge underneath is a temporary "safety" bridge built to catch falling debris.

Above: *The Panther Hollow Bridge in Schenley Park was completed in 1892. Phipps Conservatory is faintly visible in the background. Courtesy of City of Pittsburgh Department of Public Works, Bureau of Engineering and Construction. Below: Steel eyebar chain, Rachel Carson Bridge.*

BRIDGES IN THE ARTS AND EDUCATION

Above: *Carnegie Mellon University's University Center rotunda is the site of Douglas Cooper's multi-wall mural depicting Pittsburgh's topography and its bridges. The mural is 11 feet by 200 feet, charcoal on paper on board, and was completed in 1996. Courtesy of Douglas Cooper.* Below: *The design for the David L. Lawrence Convention Center was inspired by the Three Sisters bridges.*

In the case of Pittsburgh bridges not all is related to engineering as Pittsburghers celebrate their bridges in many forms of art and use them in educational studies.

The Pittsburgh Steelers training facility on the South Side features an elaborate mural celebrating noted Steelers and the City of Pittsburgh. Interestingly, the city bridges are as prominent as the various sports heroes. A more extensive and elaborate 200 foot long multi-wall mural by Douglas Cooper adorns Carnegie Mellon University's University Center rotunda walls. This mural graphically portrays the topography, bridges and neighborhoods of the city.

During 2003, artist Fred Danziger's work on a large (86" by 52") oil landscape of some of Pittsburgh's bridges over the Monongahela River, entitled *Monongahela,* was broadcast live on his Web site. Since then hc has done another pencil drawing entitled *Allegheny Study* showing a view of the Allegheny River from the Mellon (neé Civic) Arena and featuring the Fort Wayne Railroad Bridge.

The Renaissance Pittsburgh Hotel in downtown Pittsburgh has a Bridge Bar that is decorated with dramatic photographs of the city's bridges. Pittsburgh is also home to a new form of bridge art (and dare we say sport) as a collective of creative thinkers and artists began using the city's bridges as a source of inspiration. Discovering the city's bridges and renaming them based on their aesthetics became a pastime of a group fascinated by the beauty and function of the bridges. The group is known as "The Bridgespotters."

In addition to painting and photography the city's bridges are also subjects of the written and cinematic arts. A haiku by Lionel E. Deimel reads:

> *Pittsburgh, Steel City;*
> *Rivers and hills and bridges;*
> *No steel to be found.*

In 2002 the *Pittsburgh City Paper* conducted a fiction contest with the Hot Metal Bridge as the theme. The 1,000 word stories had to incorporate the bridge into their narrative by either mentioning it or having the story set wholly on the bridge.

Bridges are a vital aspect of attracting movie production companies to the 'burgh. Indeed the Pittsburgh Film Office features the city's bridges on their Web site (www.pghfilmmakers.org). In recent years the city's bridges were featured in such films as *Inspector Gadget, Cemetery Club*, and *Striking Distance*, among others. And if the city didn't have enough bridges, in 1996 a fake pedestrian bridge was built over Fifth Avenue between the Allegheny County Courthouse and One Mellon Center for the filming of *Desperate Measures* starring Pittsburgh native Michael Keaton.

Perhaps the most understated film tribute to our bridges appeared in *Wonder Boys*. According to the International Movie Database (www. imdb.com), "All key scenes feature a bridge in the background, either one of the bridges of Pittsburgh, or on a painting."

The city's bridges also inspired the design of the David L. Lawrence Convention Center (2003) located on the banks of the Allegheny River adjacent to the Three Sisters bridges. The building's architect, Rafael Viñoly, designed a structure that mirrored the grace of these bridges. In particular the shape of the roof reflects the catenary arc of the bridge suspension cables. The center is also the first 'green' convention center and the largest 'green' building in the world.

In addition to spawning artistic studies, bridges today are also being seen as art themselves. The new bridges built to relate to the environment and locales are termed signature bridges. Perhaps the most noted proponent of such bridges is the Figg Bridge Company whose display at the 2004 International Bridge Conference was entitled *Bridges as Art* and featured photographs of many of their signature bridges.

Several local teachers use the city's bridges in classroom studies. Joanne Marie Hattrup, teaching at Grandview Elementary School, developed a comprehensive program for her 3rd, 4th and 5th grade students entitled "Pittsburgh, A City of Rivers and Bridges Past and Present" that exposes them to the history, environment and wonder of the city's rivers and bridges.

Welcome to the Strip, *a mural depicting the 16th Street Bridge, can be seen on the Penn Rose building. Sandy Kessler Kaminski, Sprout Public Art, 2004.*

While obtaining research material at the Carnegie Library in Oakland, I met Geoffrey Tolge and his son David who were inquiring about some of the same material. They explained that David was working on a report on the Herr's Island Railroad Bridge for a fourth grade class project. This both amazed and intrigued me and our chance encounter led to my visiting his fourth grade class at Christ the Divine Teacher Catholic Academy in Aspinwall.

Joann Casile, who teaches social studies to fourth graders, assigned them a project on the area's bridges. Each student had to select one bridge crossing the Allegheny River, learn bridge terminology, visit and photograph the bridge, write a detailed report (complete with bibliography), and build a model of the bridge from popsicle sticks. I was amazed at the work these students did, marveled at their models, and was impressed with their knowledge of their individual bridges in particular and bridge terminology in general. David's report is reproduced in Appendix 1.

If this is representative of the work that fourth grade students are doing throughout the country then there is indeed hope for the future.

In 2004, a fifth grade class composed a group poem to the 10th Street Bridge:

Renowned 19th century sculptor Giuseppe Moretti completed numerous important public art projects in Pittsburgh including the four panthers that guard the ends of the Panther Hollow Bridge (1897) in Schenley Park. The University of Pittsburgh's Cathedral of Learning and Phipps Conservatory are in the background.

Tenth Street Bridge

A child thinks the bridge is like the laces on a giant's shoe.
The lines of the bridge are like a giant pencil.
People think the bridge is a pack of pencils pointing up
  but only one is sharp in the middle.
The bridge is as tall as my principal.
Over the bridge cars move like fast birds.
A heavy truck crosses the bridge like a football player
  tackling the receiver.
Gas from a bus smells like garbage.
A motorboat goes under the bridge like a bug in the water.
During the day the bridge hears the cars passing over it like
  thunder.
A dog on the bridge is as funny as a talking bone in the
  fridge.
A person painting the bridge looks like a dinosaur
  rebuilding itself.
The weight of the bridge feels like an elephant stomping while he is
  walking.
The feel of the steel is like my hair when I finish brushing it.
At the end of the bridge cars drive as fast as a cheetah can
  run.
The wire cables are like the afternoon sun on a sunny day.
When the sun strikes the bridge on a clear day,
  it is like turning on the lights in a theater.
The bridge sees water in the distance
  that is like glasses when they are clean.
The bridge is as yellow as the bright sun.

  The above is a group poem written by Mrs. Popp's 5th graders at Philip Murray Elementary School, January 7, 2004, during a field trip with the Pittsburgh History & Landmarks Foundation, sponsored through the South Side Local Development Company's Neighborhood Assistance Program/Comprehensive Service Program.

  And it is not only students who have composed poems about bridges. Jack Prelutsky, a noted author of children's books, composed a lyrical poem entitled *I'm Building a Bridge of Bananas* (included in *It's Raining Pigs & Noodles*), a feat even Roebling didn't attempt.

BRIDGES AND THEORETICAL MATHEMATICS

Bridges have played a role in theoretical mathematics. In this work we have used data from the city's Geographic Information System (GIS) and developed some of the maps using that technology. One of the underlying factors in the technology is *topology*. Topology is a fairly esoteric branch of mathematics that sounds strange and bewildering and is not covered in high school math studies.

However, the origin of topology is intimately related to bridges. The City of Königsburg (formerly in Germany but now called Kaliningrad and in Russia) is situated on the Pragel River. In Königsburg, the city center is an island. However, portions of the city are also located on each side of the river as well as on another nearby island downstream. All these land masses of the city, separated by the Pragel River, are connected by seven bridges.

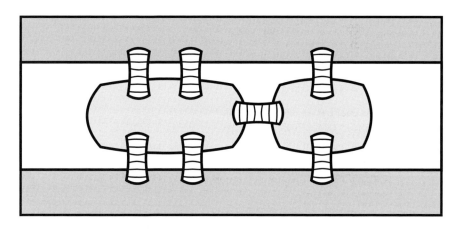

Euler's mathematical puzzle for crossing the seven bridges over Königsburg's Pragel River.

For years, the *Königsburgers* wondered if it was possible to develop a route to cross all the bridges only once and end up back where they started. There were many attempts to develop such a route but all failed. In 1735, mathematician Leonard Euler realized that all problems like this could be represented by graphing them. He replaced the areas of land by points (called vertices) and the bridges to and from them by lines (arcs). This basically was the foundation of topology and the terms *arcs* and *vertices* are still in use today.

In addition to being a city of bridges, Pittsburgh is also a center of higher education. We hope some class will revisit the Königsburg problem using Pittsburgh bridges or tunnels. (Note that there are walkways on both the Fort Pitt and Fort Duquesne Bridges.)

Oh, by the way, Euler proved that there was no such route to solve the problem, at least in Königsburg.

Opposite: *The 31st Street Bridge is owned by PennDOT and was built in 1932.*

THE BRIDGES:
A CLOSER LOOK

The confluence of the Monongahela and Allegheny rivers forming the Ohio River at what is now called the Point is one of the main reasons for the existence of Pittsburgh. Indeed, at the end of the Revolutionary War the Ohio River marked the beginning of the western frontier and the Pittsburgh area was established as one of the first gateways to the West. However, although these rivers were vitally important to the establishment of the city, so important that the Commonwealth of Pennsylvania designated certain rivers as navigable public highways, they were also impediments to the city's development.

In the early years, communication and commerce between those on all the shores of the rivers was carried out by means of private boats. In the late 1700s the first ferry service opened near the Point. Throughout the first half of the 19th century additional ferries were opened and operated. One of them crossed the Allegheny River near today's Roberto Clemente Bridge and was operated by James Robinson. His log cabin home on the North Shore was incorporated later into the seal of Allegheny City (now Pittsburgh's North Side). His son, General William Robinson for whom the street on the North Side is named, was the first non-native child born in the area and the first mayor of Allegheny City (1840). William was instrumental in bringing the Pennsylvania Railroad to the Pittsburgh area and in the establishment of the first bridge in the city across the Allegheny River (6th Street Bridge). For all his civic work, he was awarded the honorary title of General in the State Militia.

Stephan Lorant, in his book entitled *Pittsburgh: Story of an American City*, describes river crossings at that time:

> *On the river below the Point, passengers still had to cross by means of ferries, and winter ice, summer sand bars, and slow-moving strings of coal barges made ferry travel both hazardous and tedious.*

Bridge building began during the early 19th century, ultimately leading to the demise of the ferries. The first bridge across the Monongahela River was the original Smithfield Street Bridge, a wooden covered toll bridge built in 1818. The first St. Clair (6th Street) Bridge crossed the Allegheny River the following year. By the 1850s there were five bridges across the Allegheny River and two across the Monongahela River. Bridge building hasn't stopped since that time.

It was not only the rivers but also the surrounding terrain that had to be tamed for transportation purposes. In doing so, Pittsburghers resorted to using steps, inclines, tunnels and bridges. There seems to be bridges everywhere, and although London Bridge is now in Arizona, all the Pittsburgh bridges are still here or, in some cases, nearby.

In this section, we briefly examine our city's most famous bridges, detail some bridges unique to Pittsburgh, and explore some less known structures. As an aside, there may be differences by a year or so in the reported date for a bridge due to the fact that it takes several years to complete construction. Some sources cite the year the bridge was spanned, some the year completed, and some the year opened.

16th Street Bridge detail.

THE BIG 'UNS

View of bridges up the Monongahela River taken from Mount Washington. Starting with the Smithfield Street Bridge in the foreground bottom left are the Panhandle (light rail), Liberty, South 10th Street, and at the top center, the Birmingham.

Within, or at, the city limits there are 29 big bridges (The Big 'uns) spanning the Allegheny, the Monongahela and the Ohio rivers. Six of these carry rail or light rail, one is now a pedestrian/bicycle bridge and another will soon join this latter category. These bridges are listed in table opposite.

The West End Bridge spans the Ohio River; it opened in 1932.

The Big 'uns		
	Name (Date)	**Current Owner**
Ohio River	Ohio River Connecting Railroad (1915)	CSX
	McKees Rocks Bridge (1931)	PennDOT
	West End Bridge (1932)	PennDOT
Allegheny River	Fort Duquesne (main span built in 1963, completed in 1969)	PennDOT
	Roberto Clemente (6th Street) (1928)	County
	Andy Warhol (7th Street) (1926)	County
	Rachel Carson (9th Street) (1927)	County
	Fort Wayne Railroad (1904)	Norfolk & Southern Railroad
	Veterans (1987)	PennDOT
	16th Street (1923)	County
	Herr's (Heir's) Island Railroad (now Three Rivers Heritage Trail) (1903)	City
	Herr's (Heir's) Island Backchannel (1986)	City
	33rd Street Railroad (1928)	PennDOT
	31st Street Bridge (1927)	PennDOT
	40th Street (Washington Crossing) (1924)	PennDOT
	R. D. Fleming (62nd Street) (1962)	PennDOT
	Highland Park (1938)	PennDOT
	Brilliant Branch Railroad (1904)	Allegheny Valley Railroad
Monongahela River	Fort Pitt (opened 1959)	PennDOT
	Smithfield Street (1883)	PennDOT
	Monongahela River Bridge (Panhandle/light rail) (1904)	Port Authority
	Liberty (1927)	PennDOT
	South 10th Street (1931)	County
	Birmingham (1977)	PennDOT
	Hot Metal (1900)	City
	Monongahela Connecting Railroad (1904)	City
	Glenwood (1966)	County
	Glenwood-B&O Railroad Bridge (1915)	B&O Railroad
	Homestead Grays (High Level) (1936)	County

The Big 'uns are the focus of, and detailed in, many of the articles and books on the bridges of this area. However, it is still worthwhile to call attention to a few of them.

THE THREE SISTERS

The Roberto Clemente, Andy Warhol and Rachel Carson bridges spanning the Allegheny River and connecting downtown to the North Side are the *only* three identical side-by-side bridges in the world and are known collectively as "The Three Sisters", although two are now named after men. They are also occasionally referred to as the "Trinity of Bridges." The three are all of a unique design: self-anchored suspension bridges with a large steel eyebar suspension system. The next time you cross one notice how the cables resemble a chain on a bicycle. They are also unusual in that they were constructed using cantilever methods. According to Thomas Donatelli, Director of Public Works for Allegheny County (owner of The Three Sisters), the only other example of this design is in Cologne, Germany.

The Allegheny County Bureau of Bridges headed by George Richardson, built these bridges in the late 1920s; Stanley Roush of the department was the architect. This period immediately prior to the Great Depression was an unprecedented era of bridge building activities in the city and county. Fortunately, all designs were done in concert with the Art Commission and all included had a feeling for the aesthetic as well as practical aspects of bridge building. A recognition of this came when the (then) 6th Street Bridge was declared the "Most Beautiful Steel Bridge of 1928" by the American Institute of Steel Construction.

The Three Sisters—two of which are now ironically named after men—are the only three identical side-by-side bridges in the world.

Below: *Fans of Andy Warhol celebrated along with Councilman Doug Shields (left) and Andy Warhol Museum Director Tom Sokolowski as the 7th Street Bridge was renamed in Warhol's honor on March 18, 2005.*

Note the suspension cables anchoring the Roberto Clemente Bridge.

What's In A Name?

These bridges or their predecessors at the same locations have borne different names throughout time. The Clemente Bridge was the 6th Street Bridge, and prior to that the St. Clair Street Bridge. The Warhol Bridge was formerly known as 7th Street and before that the Federal Street Bridge, and the Rachel Carson Bridge was called the 9th Street and the Hand Street Bridge.

Dave Copeland, writing in the *Pittsburgh Tribune-Review* on October 6, 2003, noted that these and all the major bridges in the downtown area are painted the same color, Aztec gold. He also reported that City Councilman William Peduto would like to see the 7th Street Bridge painted ultraviolet purple and named after native son Andy Warhol whose namesake museum is at the northern end of the bridge. In addition, Mr. Peduto suggested that the 9th Street Bridge be painted green and named for environmentalist Rachel Carson. Part of the councilman's wish came true in November 2004 when Allegheny County Council voted to rename the 7th Street Bridge in honor of Andy Warhol. The formal name dedication occurred on March 18, 2005, complete with a day-long celebration on the bridge. And in December of 2005, Council voted to change the name of the 9th Street Bridge to the Rachel Carson Bridge.

Smithfield Street Bridge designed by Gustav Lindenthal. Courtesy of the Photo Antiquities Archives.

The arch-design 40th Street Bridge connecting Lawrenceville to Millvale is also known as the Washington Crossing Bridge and marks the most likely spot where George Washington and Christopher Gist crossed

DEDICATED BY THE
CHRISTOPHER GIST CHAPTER
OF THE
DAUGHTERS OF THE AMERICAN
COLONIST'S 2003.

IN 1753
GEORGE WASHINGTON AND HIS GUIDE,
CHRISTOPHER GIST, CROSSED THE
ALLEGHENY RIVER AT THIS SITE.

THEIR JOURNEY WOULD TAKE THEM TO
FORT LE BOEUF, NEAR PRESENT DAY ERIE
WITH A LAST REQUEST FOR THE
FRENCH TO LEAVE THE TERRITORY.
THE FRENCH AND INDIAN WAR
WOULD SOON FOLLOW.

the Allegheny River in 1753 returning from a mission to the French. This bridge is noted for the seals of the thirteen original states that adorn the railings. A covered wooden bridge previously occupied this site. The 33rd Street Railroad Bridge is in the background (opposite page).

GEORGE WASHINGTON
A MESSENGER FROM THE GOVERNOR OF VIRGINIA TO THE
COMMANDANT OF THE FRENCH FORCES ON THE OHIO
AND CHRISTOPHER GIST, HIS GUIDE
CROSSED THE ALLEGHENY RIVER AT THIS POINT
ON DECEMBER 29, 1753
ON THE RETURN JOURNEY FROM FORT LE BOEUF

PLACED BY THE PITTSBURGH CHAPTER
DAUGHTERS OF THE AMERICAN REVOLUTION
1926

Construction on the cantilever-style East Street Bridge began in 1929; it is known as the Gateway Arch of the North Hills. Photo courtesy of City of Pittsburgh Department of Public Works, Bureau of Engineering and Construction.

SMITHFIELD STREET BRIDGE

The Smithfield Street Bridge spanning the Monongahela River near Station Square is a bridge of legends. The present bridge, delicately and faithfully restored in 1995, is the oldest extant bridge in the city, and was built in 1883. The location is appropriate, considering that this was the first site of a river crossing bridge, and also the site of a bridge built by the famous engineer John Roebling. The first bridge was a wooden covered toll bridge built in 1818 that was destroyed by fire. The second bridge (Roebling's), built in 1846, was an iron suspension bridge. A Pennsylvania Historical and Museum Commission marker honoring Roebling is beside the bridge at the Station Square end. His bridge was not destroyed by fire, but rather condemned as increasing traffic and loads caused the bridge to shake excessively. The current bridge was designed by Gustav Lindenthal (page 71).

PANHANDLE BRIDGE

The so-called Panhandle Bridge (the official name is the Monongahela River Bridge) was built in 1903 for the Pittsburgh and Steubenville Railroad Company. This railroad served the "panhandle" of West Virginia

The 16th Street Bridge just upriver from the Three Sisters was built in 1928 and completely refurbished to its original grandeur in 2003. It is noteworthy in that it replaced the last wooden bridge in the city. The original 16th Street, or Mechanic Street Bridge (or the Upper Bridge) as it was then known, was a covered wooden bridge that burned several times, most recently in 1919.

and thus the nickname for the bridge. Trains crossing the bridge into the city entered a railroad tunnel that ultimately led them to Union Station. The Port Authority acquired the bridge in the early 1980s and it has been in service as a light rail transit bridge since 1985.

If one looks at the bridge's stone piers, especially on the south end, a change of color can be seen. This is due to the fact that the bridge had to be raised when flood control was initiated on the Monongahela River in 1913.

SOUTH 10TH STREET BRIDGE

The South 10th Street Bridge traversing the Monongahela River connects Second Avenue to the South Side (photo page 41). Although similar in appearance to the Three Sisters bridges, it is different and worthy of notice as it is the *only* true wire suspension bridge in the City of Pittsburgh. The wire rope splays into individual wires under the ground at both ends of the bridge and is deeply anchored in concrete blocks.

A LONE BIG 'UN

It has been reported that a writer for the *New York Times* described Pittsburgh as "the only city in America with an entrance," alluding to the spectacular view afforded in approaching the city through the Fort Pitt Tunnel. However, if one approaches the city from the north via I-279, one realizes that the city has another grand entrance. It is not a backdoor, either, as the view of the city after passing the E. H. Swindell (East Street) Bridge is similarly spectacular. This bridge, built in 1930 (60 years before I-279), is often called the "Gateway Arch of the North Hills." This undoubtedly refers to the appearance when one is traveling north. However, it similarly could be called the "Gateway to Pittsburgh" for those traveling south.

For those interested, it is a cantilever style bridge. Utilizing what White noted about the difference between cantilever and arch construction, this is readily apparent as the bridge would still stand if the centerpiece were removed (photo page 74).

HISTORIC BIG 'UNS

This aerial photo taken before 1970 shows the Fort Pitt Bridge (near-left) and the Fort Duquesne Bridge near-right; the old Point Bridge #2 and Manchester bridges (mid-left and-right respectively) were subsequently torn down. The West End Bridge is just visible at the top of the photo; construction for Three Rivers Stadium can be seen mid-right between the two bridges across the Allegheny River. Photo courtesy of the Library and Archives Division, Historical Society of Western Pennsylvania, Pittsburgh, PA.

The present day Big 'uns have a long ancestry with many predecessors. These historic Big 'uns are listed in the table on the following page.

The history of bridges in the City of Pittsburgh basically is the story of these proud structures and we highlight a few noteworthy ones.

The Point

The Point, which has played such a pivotal role in the history of the City of Pittsburgh, is also the locale of much bridge history. Although it seems like a natural site for a bridge, it was not until 1875, or more than a half a century after the first river crossing bridge, that a bridge first touched the shores at the Point. Over the next century four different bridges would occupy a portion of the Point. Although all are gone, remnants of two still remain, one clearly visible near Heinz Field and the other, less so, on the southern side of the Monongahela near the Station Square access road, and usually obscured by barges.

The first bridge at the Point was a wooden covered toll bridge called the Union Bridge, which spanned the Allegheny River from the end of the Point to the area near Heinz Field. It had many piers or supports and was quite low to the water. Years ago, before flood controls (dams) were established, the three rivers were quite shallow and not readily

This 1912 photo shows the Point Bridge river pier and the Exposition Park roller coaster. Photo courtesy of City of Pittsburgh Department of Public Works, Bureau of Engineering and Construction.

Historic Big 'uns		
	Name	Date
Allegheny River	Union (covered bridge) *	1875-1907
	Manchester	1915-1970
	6th (St. Clair Street) #1 (covered bridge; first bridge over Allegheny) *	1819-1857
	6th (St. Clair Street) #2	1857-1892
	6th Street (St. Clair Street) #3	1892-1927
	7th Street	1885-1925
	9th Street (Hand Street) (covered bridge) *	1839-1890
	9th Street	1890-1925
	Fort Wayne Railroad	1857-1868
	Fort Wayne Railroad	1868-1904
	Pennsylvania (Allegheny) Canal #1	1829-1845
	Pennsylvania (Allegheny) Canal #2	1845-1857
	16th Street (Mechanic Street) (covered bridge) *	1838-1923
	16th Street	1851-1919
	Herr's Island—30th Street	1882-1887
		1887-1921
		1921-1927
	Herr's Island—backchannel	1939-1986
	33rd Street Railroad	1884
	43rd Street (Ewald Street)	1870-1924
	Highland Park	c. 1902-1938
Monongahela River	Point Bridge #1	1877-1927
	Point Bridge #2	1927-1970
	Wabash Railroad	1902-1948
	Monongahela Bridge (Smithfield Street) (covered bridge) *	1818-1845
	Monongahela Suspension Bridge (Smithfield Street)	1846-1881
	Panhandle Railroad	1865-1903
	South 10th Street (Birmingham) *	1861-1875
	South 10th Street (Birmingham)	1904-1931
	South 22nd Street (Brady Street)	1895-1977
* denotes wooden bridges		

navigable by large boats. However, this changed, and with the higher river level, the Union Bridge became a liability and an impediment to river traffic.

The Union Bridge was replaced in 1915 by the Manchester Bridge, so named because that was the original name of a borough established in 1843 (in contrast to Birmingham, on the South Side). In 1867 Manchester was merged into and became a neighborhood in Allegheny City, now Pittsburgh's North Side. Manchester Beach was a popular swimming area on the shore of the Ohio River located not far from the north end of the bridge at the end of Franklin Street. The bridge was a well ornamented "through truss" bridge that serviced vehicular and street railway traffic until its destruction in 1970. The large pier located near Heinz Field belonged to this bridge, and some of its ornaments, historic figures, are located across the street from the Pittsburgh Children's Museum.

The first bridge at the Point across the Monongahela River was built in 1877 and was a suspension bridge known only as Point Bridge #1. A photo sure to evoke *deja vu* (adding perhaps, in considering what

The newly constructed North Portal of the Manchester Bridge, December 2, 1918. Photo courtesy of City of Pittsburgh Department of Public Works, Bureau of Engineering and Construction.

Point Bridge #1 is visible in the foreground; Manchester Bridge is in the background. Just beyond the Manchester Bridge you can see Exposition Park, original home of the Pittsburgh Pirates and site of the first World Series game. Photo courtesy of Carnegie Library of Pittsburgh.

it shows, the words of Yogi Berra—"all over again") is the Manchester Bridge and this first Point Bridge (above). The *deja vu* part comes when one notices the baseball park on the North Side remarkably close to the present day PNC Park.

This was Exposition Park, original home of today's Pittsburgh Pirates and site of the first World Series game. An analysis of historic maps reveals that it was almost at the same location as Three Rivers Stadium. Prior to the ballpark, Exposition Park had been a racetrack. Exposition Park was also used as a name for buildings and amusement rides located on the Point itself. The photo on page 78 shows the Point Bridge pier and a roller coaster at this Exposition Park on the Point.

Point Bridge #1 was replaced by Point Bridge #2 which was built next to it and slightly upstream in 1927. This contemporary of the Manchester Bridge was also a "through truss" style that carried vehicular and street railway traffic until 1959. However, it was not dismantled until the same year as the Manchester Bridge (1970) when the Point, as we know it, was being developed.

82   *The Bridges of Pittsburgh*

ALLEGHENY (PENNSYLVANIA) CANAL BRIDGE

A wooden aqueduct was built across the Allegheny River in 1836. The structure carried the Pennsylvania Canal across the River to the northern end of a tunnel that then carried the canal under Grant Hill to the shores of the Monongahela River. It was located near present-day 11th Street, not far from the Fort Wayne Railroad and Veterans bridges.

This wooden aqueduct, formally known as the Allegheny Canal Bridge, was removed in 1845 to make way for the world's first wire suspension bridge (built by John Roebling).

In 1861 a portion of the bridge sagged and the bridge was closed, stranding two canal boats in the City of Pittsburgh. After repairs and with the infusion once again of water, a section collapsed and the bridge was abandoned and ultimately torn down. In proving the old adage that if at first you don't succeed, try again, Roebling went on to perfect his wire rope suspension system and to build two more bridges in

All that remains of the Wabash Railroad Bridge are the abutments, one of which is shown in the lower portion of the photo to the left of the Gateway Clipper boat.

Pittsburgh (Smithfield Street and St. Clair Street bridges) as well as the Niagara Gorge and Brooklyn bridges.

WABASH RAILROAD BRIDGE

The Wabash Railroad Bridge, built in 1904, was one of the longest cantilever railroad bridges in the United States. It belonged to the Wabash-Pittsburgh Terminal Railroad (the "Wabash"). The bridge carried the railroad from the Wabash Tunnel across the Monongahela River to the Wabash Building, located on the site of the present-day Gateway Center "T" station. The bridge was dismantled in 1948 and the steel reused in the construction of the Dravosburg Bridge. The piers, one on each side of the Monongahela River, still remain as a reminder of this majestic bridge.

BRADY STREET BRIDGE

The old Brady Street Bridge, also called the South 22nd Street Bridge, spanned the Monongahela River from 1895 until 1977. It was the first river bridge in the city built to be toll free. The photo below shows this bridge and its replacement, the Birmingham Bridge, revealing a sharp contrast in bridge design in the 82 years between the two. The Brady Street Bridge is gone but not forgotten as railings from this bridge adorn the lower section of the Monongahela Incline.

The Brady Street Bridge (left) was torn down in 1977 to make way for the Birmingham Bridge (right). Photo courtesy of the Carnegie Library of Pittsburgh.

Above: *Demolition of the Point Bridge #1, 1927. Courtesy of City of Pittsburgh Department of Public Works, Bureau of Engineering and Construction.* Below: *A major flood in 1964 crested at 31.64 feet. The outline of Fort Duquesne is just visible in Point State Park. Floods such as these often create damage to the area's bridges and were especially damaging prior to flood control measures being implemented on the rivers. Photo courtesy of the Library and Archives Division, Historical Society of Western Pennsylvania, Pittsburgh, PA.*

Some Lesser Known Bridges

Drawing for the Murray Avenue Bridge, 1912. Courtesy of City of Pittsburgh Department of Public Works, Bureau of Engineering and Construction.

A residential street, Hoeveler, named in honor of a prominent East Liberty businessman, was dramatically altered during urban renewal and basically replaced by East Liberty Boulevard. A beautiful arch bridge, known as the Hoeveler Street Bridge, was located between Larimer Avenue and Collins Street on today's East Liberty Boulevard. The bridge was built in 1912 and demolished in 1968 in the name of progress.

Another bridge, the only remnants of which are stone abutments, carried Ellsworth Avenue across today's East Busway to intersect with Centre Avenue. The bridge built in 1908 was located at the intersection of Ellsworth Avenue and Spahr Street; the rise in the road at this juncture bears mute testament to this long gone bridge. Beside the bridge was a pedestrian bridge also crossing the railroad and leading to Sacred Heart Church and School, then located on Centre Avenue where the Whole Foods store is today. In early 2005, East Liberty Development, Inc. received a $1,000,000 grant from the state to reestablish this pedestrian bridge.

Above: *California Avenue Bridge and Steps, 1929.* Below: *Castor Street Bridge, 1918. Courtesy of City of Pittsburgh Department of Public Works, Bureau of Engineering and Construction.*

Above: *Atherton Avenue (Baum Boulevard) Bridge over the Pittsburgh Junction Railroad, 1913. Note the Luna Park roller coaster behind the bridge (middle-left) in the top of the photo.* Below: *The Kearns Street Bridge, 1908. Courtesy of City of Pittsburgh Department of Public Works, Bureau of Engineering and Construction.*

The Mission Street Bridge in 1924 (above) and during dismantling in 1939 (below). Courtesy of City of Pittsburgh Department of Public Works, Bureau of Engineering and Construction.

Railroad Bridges

Trains pass in opposite directions on the Ohio Connecting Railroad Bridge over the Ohio River.

In contrast to the many aesthetically pleasing bridges throughout the city, there are the many utilitarian, uniformly black, railroad bridges. Although many are spectacular, such as the river crossings, the high trestles, and the Brilliant Cutoff Viaduct, most are aesthetically drab. In looking at all the railroad bridges in the city, the only ones that don't look like railroad bridges are those over East Street or parts of I-279, under, or near, the Veterans Bridge. They are distinguishable from the nearby bridges only by the chain link fences that adorn them.

The older railroad bridges were all designed and built to carry very heavy loads. Close examination of them reveals that they were overbuilt by many bridge standards. Also, the older ones were riveted, and thus not as prone to fatigue as are many of the modern welded bridges. They are uniformly black, painted years ago with long-lasting coal tar bituminous paint. Such a coating could not be used with today's environmental restrictions. Indeed, one of the biggest problems associated with renewing bridges is the environmental restrictions involved in removing the older coats of paint. The protective draping of the northern ends of the Fort Duquesne Bridge during this process in 2004 provided mute testimony to this aspect of bridge renewal (photo page 37).

Another reason for the durability of the railroad bridges is that they never have to endure salting, which is the most corrosive problem facing modern bridges. The only railroad bridge in the city that suffered the ravages of salt is the lower deck of the Fort Wayne Railroad Bridge. This bridge located near the Convention Center was built by the Fort Wayne and Chicago Railway Company. The lower portion of the bridge led to the Strip District and refrigerated cars of that era relied on ice and brine for cooling. The leakage of the brine over many years deteriorated this portion of the bridge. Studies by the Port Authority showed that it would be cheaper to traverse the Allegheny River by tunnel rather than to rehabilitate this portion of the bridge because the deterioration is so severe.

Located just off Washington Boulevard is the Brilliant Cutoff Viaduct (photo page 9). This 75 foot high multi-arched railroad bridge, named in reference to that section of the Pennsylvania Railroad between East Liberty and Aspinwall, is eerily reminiscent of the many stone arch bridges constructed by the Roman Empire. When one views this stone arch bridge and the adjacent Lincoln Avenue Viaduct, one feels immediately transported back in time.

The Brilliant Cutoff Viaduct was constructed in 1903 and when the City of Pittsburgh built the Lincoln Avenue Bridge several years later it did so in a manner to blend with the railroad bridge design. Historic postcards show that this was a particularly scenic site when Silver Lake, once at the junction of these two bridges, was still extant.

PEDESTRIAN BRIDGES

One of Schenley Park's several tufa bridges.

Pittsburgh's pedestrian bridges are not pedestrian in their design or building. There are approximately 40 pedestrian bridges scattered throughout the city. This count does not include private bridges, such as those owned by the University of Pittsburgh over Forbes Avenue or the one crossing Penn Avenue near Stanwix Street, but rather those owned and maintained by the various public entities.

WILKSBORO AVENUE FOOTBRIDGE

The Wilksboro Avenue Footbridge is a spectacular trestle-like structure in the Brighton Heights section of the city's North Side. It was originally called the Wheeler Avenue Footbridge when this area was still Allegheny City prior to its annexation by the City of Pittsburgh in 1907. Built at a cost of $3,060 in 1895, repaired in 1917 and 1953, it is a 370-foot long steel beam footbridge with a maximum depth between the bridge deck and valley floor of 105 feet. It is now in need of extensive work although still spectacular to behold. In the 1970s, the bridge was temporarily shut down while a Volkswagen Beetle was extricated and in 1977, motorcycle barriers were also erected.

Journalist Brian O'Neill, in his inimitable fashion, gave a vivid portrayal of this bridge in a June 27, 2004 article in the *Pittsburgh Post-Gazette*, recounting not only the Beetle incident but also the importance of the bridge to the neighborhood and our heritage. Noting that the bridge still stands primarily because the city doesn't have the money to tear it down, O'Neill goes on to lament, "I keep thinking that previous generations left Pittsburgh with all this cool stuff, and here we are, saving up just to throw treasures away."

Wilksboro Avenue is between Termon Avenue and California Avenue.

WINDGAP SUSPENSION BRIDGE

The Windgap Suspension Bridge spans Chartiers Creek, connecting the Windgap/Esplen area in the West End of the city with McKees Rocks. It was constructed in 1919 on the foundations of an older bridge dating back to the mid-1800s. It is a dramatic suspension bridge with a wooden plank deck. Unfortunately, it was damaged in the 2004 flood, but is firmly in the county's budget with plans for a complete rehabilitation.

A favorite pastime of many generations of local teens is to get in the middle of the bridge and shake it as hard as they can. The bridge is located at the end of Township Road off Youghiogheny Road which, when heading towards McKees Rocks, is the last turn off Windgap Road before the Windgap Bridge.

SCHENLEY PARK TUFA BRIDGES

Perhaps some of the most picturesque pedestrian bridges in the city are those located on the trails throughout Schenley Park. Of particular

Text continues on page 98.

Right: *Definitely worth a visit, the Wilksboro Avenue Footbridge is a spectacular trestle-like structure in the Brighton Heights section of the North Side. It was first built in 1895. Below: Detail of the structure.*

*The Windgap Suspension Bridge spans Chartiers Creek
in the city's western portion. It was built in 1919.*

Although not in the tally of bridges, private bridges are plentiful in the city. Above: *This private pedestrian bridge spans Forbes Avenue in Oakland and is owned by the University of Pittsburgh.* Below: *This private pedestrian bridge crosses Penn Avenue near Stanwix in downtown Pittsburgh.*

INTERSTATE HIGHWAY FOOTBRIDGES

It should also be noted that while it is rare to have pedestrian walkways *on* interstate highway bridges, Pittsburgh has two: the well-known broad walkway from the Point to the North Shore on the Fort Duquesne Bridge and a lesser known (and narrower) walkway from the Point to West Carson Street on the Fort Pitt Bridge.

Two noteworthy pedestrian bridges are those that *cross* two interstate highways: Gerst Way (right), a former street, but now a pedestrian bridge over the Parkway North (I-279), and below and on the next page, the bridge that carries a portion of a set of city steps over the Parkway East (I-376). Sad to say, this unique feature connecting us to our historic past has been deemed an eyesore and is slated for demolition rather than reconstruction and preservation.

Right: *Gerst Way.*

Below: *Close-up detail from the opposite page.*

The Parkway East bridge and steps in Oakland are visible to the left (1) in this aerial photo taken in 1984; the steps cross the Parkway East and Second Avenue below it (2). The Jones & Laughlin Steel Company mills at the upper left (3) of the photo fronting the Monongahela River were torn down in the 1980s and replaced in the 1990s by high tech office buildings. The former Monongahela Connecting Railroad Bridge is now open to vehicular traffic and the Hot Metal Bridge next to it is expected to open to pedestrians and cyclists in the next few years (4). Photo courtesy of Pittsburgh Department of City Planning.

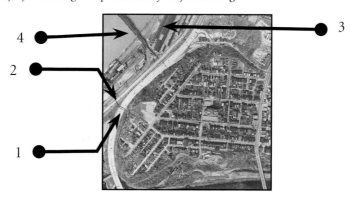

interest are the *tufa bridges* built in 1908 along the then bridle (now hiking) trail, but still known as the Lower Panther Hollow Bridle Trail.

The tufa coating of these reinforced concrete arch bridges gives them a unique, picturesque and distinctive appearance. Tufa is an unusually attractive calcium carbonate rock that typically forms on limestone cliffs, quarry outcroppings, or caves when the limestone interacts with water and the water evaporates. The most spectacular occurrences of tufa are the coral-like "Tufa Towers" of Mono Lake, California. However, the tufa of the Schenley Park bridges is fittingly more pedestrian, having come from Ohio.

HISTORIC PEDESTRIAN BRIDGES

Like their big brothers, the pedestrian bridges of Pittsburgh also have some historic ancestors. Although these are not documented in the text, several are preserved photographically in the archives of the city's Department of Public Works, Bureau of Engineering and Construction. Of particular interest are some of the earlier wooden pedestrian bridges. These, along with some other historic footbridges are shown in the following pages.

Above: *The Timberland Footbridge spanning Saw Mill Run shown in 1909.* Below: *Timberland Avenue Bridge over West Side Belt RR looking east. Courtesy of City of Pittsburgh Department of Public Works, Bureau of Engineering and Construction.*

Above: *This photo taken in 1930 shows a long-gone footbridge spanning the railroad tracks in front of Penn Station.* Below: *Detail from photo showing footbridge. Courtesy of City of Pittsburgh Department of Public Works, Bureau of Engineering and Construction.*

Above and below: *The McFarren Avenue Footbridge in the foreground above and below, and Brown's Bridge, forerunner to the Homestead High Level Bridge, is in the background above (1936 above and undated below). Courtesy of City of Pittsburgh Department of Public Works, Bureau of Engineering and Construction.*

Above: *The Oregon Avenue Footbridge, 1919.* Below: *The Duquesne Incline Footbridge over Carson Street in 1932; this bridge is still in use. Courtesy of City of Pittsburgh Department of Public Works, Bureau of Engineering and Construction.*

Tunnels

(NEGATIVE BRIDGES)

Previous page: *The long-closed Wabash Tunnel was re-opened in 2004 to help alleviate traffic between downtown Pittsburgh and the South Hills.*

Above: *Fort Pitt Tunnel with upper deck-level foggy view of Fort Pitt Bridge.*
Below: *Emerging from the Liberty Tunnels onto the Liberty Bridge.*

An alternative to bridging the gaps in the terrain is to burrow through high standing obstacles and that the city has done in spades. A subtitle to the name "City of Bridges" could be "City of Tunnels" as there are 11 major tunnels in the city and several minor ones (pedestrian, bridge approaches). Perhaps in this context, tunnels could be called negative bridges.

In late 2004 Pittsburgh saw the reopening of one of the oldest tunnels in the city—the Wabash Tunnel. Long the butt of jokes and complementing the Bridge to Nowhere (see page 107) as the Tunnel to Nowhere, it had among many suggestions been considered as a locale to set a record in bowling for the longest strike ever. However, the former railroad tunnel, now owned by the Port Authority, was finally reopened to vehicular traffic.

Unfortunately for those who suffer from a fear of bridges it has been shown that they are also likely to develop a fear of tunnels (claustrophobia). However as all drivers in the city know, it is not this fear which

This train tunnel, shown at the Boundary Street end in Oakland, is owned by CSXT Railroad and runs under Neville Avenue all the way to Baum Boulevard.

prompts tunnel traffic but rather the basic feeling of loss of light, space and air prompting all drivers to slow down in tunnels. Fortunately, there is light at the end of the tunnel (so to speak) as some work has finally started on the design of psychologically correct structures in which color, light and tunnel widths are altered to help alleviate this distress. While this won't solve the biggest cause of congestion—too many vehicles on the roads—it may help relieve the problem of backed-up traffic. Anyone crossing the Fort Pitt Bridge and entering the tunnel would undoubtedly appreciate any help available.

Unique Pittsburgh Bridges

The Underground Bridge: Bellefield Bridge with Forbes Field in the background. This bridge is now completely underground. Library of Congress Prints and Photographs Division, Detroit Publishing Company Collection, [reproduction number: LC-D4-39105].

In keeping with the character of the city, there are several bridges that are undoubtedly unique and worthy of attention.

Bridge to Nowhere

The Fort Duquesne Bridge became known as "The Bridge to Nowhere" when the main structure was completed in 1963 but the north side access ramps were left undone due to discussions about how and where these would be located. It wasn't until six years later that the ramps were completed and the bridge opened to traffic.

In the meantime, the bridge was perfectly accessible, although barricaded, from one end (the south) but with a deck terminating in open space several stories above the North Shore. The bridge gained great notoriety when in late 1964 a University of Pittsburgh student drove through the barricades across the bridge and off the north end. Fortunately, he landed without major injury.

The Fort Duquesne Bridge is one of many throughout the United States that at one time or another bore the name "Bridge to Nowhere." The most famous of these was undoubtedly the Hoan Bridge in Milwaukee. Built in 1970 it was not completed until the late seventies, and even then not all ramps were completed. Its notoriety derives from its appearance in the 1980 film, *The Blues Brothers*. In a classic scene (eerily familiar to our Pitt student), a red Pinto is shown driving off the end of the unfinished bridge. In true Hollywood fashion the car was never driven off the bridge, but rather dropped from a helicopter for the following scene showing car and occupants falling to earth.

If you look carefully at the southern end of the Birmingham Bridge you will notice that Pittsburgh still has a mini "bridge to nowhere" as there are two unfinished connecting ramps leading to open space. The southern end of the bridge is symmetric with the north end except that two off-ramps were never completed. This probably is due to the fact that the bridge was built as part of a plan for an inner-city belt highway that never materialized.

UNDERGROUND BRIDGE

The Oakland area of Pittsburgh contains a beautiful stone arch bridge that is completely functional, except that it is buried deep underground. The area that long hosted a parking lot and is bounded by the Carnegie Library, Hillman Library and Forbes Avenue was once a deep ravine known as Saint Pierre's. The Bellefield Bridge was built in 1898 to cross this ravine at the southern end, providing access to Schenley Park. Seventeen years later, there were plans to develop a grand entrance to Schenley Park, and the ravine, complete with bridge, was filled in.

Today, the bridge (probably the best preserved bridge in the city requiring the least maintenance) lies completely undisturbed beneath the Mary Schenley Fountain in front of the University of Pittsburgh's Frick Fine Arts Building. Once again it will be a silent witness to renewed efforts to provide a fitting entrance to bucolic Schenley Park as the former parking lot has been converted into a park-like setting.

BRIDGE THAT IS BEING BURIED

The Haight's (Heth's) Run ravine over which the Haight's Run Bridge carries Butler Street near the Pittsburgh Zoo parking lot has been filled

Above: *Haight's (Heth's) Run Bridge during construction in 1914.* Below: *Drawing for the bridge done in 1912. Courtesy of City of Pittsburgh Department of Public Works, Bureau of Engineering and Construction.*

in to a great extent. The natural forces that are at work continue to infill the ravine, gradually turning the bridge into a roadway.

The 1914 photo and construction drawing above of this attractive bridge shows it under construction. The original Highland Park Bridge

*This dramatic view from Mount Washington looking up the Monongahela
River is a tourism magnet and an invitation to explore the city's bridges.*

(1902—ca. 1938) is in the background. This view is from the south-
eastern end of the bridge. The original Highland Park Bridge, of which
there are few records, was not at the same location as the present bridge
but rather approximately 2,000 feet downstream toward the Point. It
connected Baker Street with 19th Street in Sharpsburg.

Two in one bridge

Pittsburghers often refer to the Hot Metal Bridge, and many drive
across it. Yet the bridge carrying today's vehicular traffic is not the Hot
Metal Bridge, but rather the Monongahela Connecting Railroad Bridge.
The Hot Metal Bridge is the unused bridge next to it on the downstream side. In 1887 there was one bridge at this site. During 1899-1900
the piers were expanded and the Hot Metal Bridge constructed. In 1904
the present day Monongahela Connecting Railroad Bridge was built to
replace the original bridge as the company determined that it would

View of the Hot Metal Bridge looking north with the Monongahela Connecting Bridge to the left. Note the guard panels on the right which protected river traffic below from molten metal. William Samek, 1993. Library of Congress Prints and Photographs Division [reproduction number: HAER, PA,2-PITBU,65C-4].

have been too costly to strengthen the original single track structure to carry the steadily increasing loads.

This Hot Metal Bridge was one of three that crossed the Monongahela River with the others located at Homestead and Rankin. It carried molten iron (hot metal) produced in the blast furnaces on the north side of the river at the Jones and Laughlin Steel Co. to J & L's open hearth furnaces on the South Side. Twenty-four trains a day consisting of an engine, two "torpedo" cars, and a caboose crossed the bridge. The bridge ceased use for this purpose in 1979 when the open hearth furnaces were replaced by electric arc furnaces. The bridge was then used as a utility bridge, i.e., to carry various utility lines.

Plans are in the works to refurbish the actual Hot Metal Bridge as a pedestrian/bike bridge to connect the rail-trails that run along both sides of the river.

The former (third) Saint Clair Street (6th Street) Bridge, dismantled and making its way down the Ohio to its new home over the Ohio from Coraopolis to Neville Island. Courtesy Carnegie Library of Pittsburgh.

RECYCLED BRIDGE

To make way for today's Roberto Clemente Bridge, the third Saint Clair Street (6th Street) Bridge was recycled in 1927 rather than destroyed. A new bridge was needed between Coraopolis and Neville Island, and Allegheny County determined that it could save money by dismantling this structure, moving it, and reassembling it at the new location. Accordingly, each 440 foot long, 44 foot wide, 80 foot high, 1600 ton truss floated merrily down the Allegheny and Ohio rivers to its new home where the various pieces were re-assembled.

BRIDGE THAT IS A BUILDING

One of Pittsburgh's most famous bridges is not a bridge at all but rather a part of a famous building designed by H. H. Richardson. The "Bridge of Sighs", spanning Ross Street and connecting the old county jail with the county courthouse, is not considered a bridge by the county but rather a part of a building. The bridge got its name from the sadness prisoners felt (or were thought to feel) when led from the courthouse to the jail. The jail, by the way, has been readapted into a home for Family Court.

BRIDGE IN A BUILDING

At one time, the Pennsylvania Canal ran through a tunnel beneath the downtown section of the City of Pittsburgh. A railroad tunnel

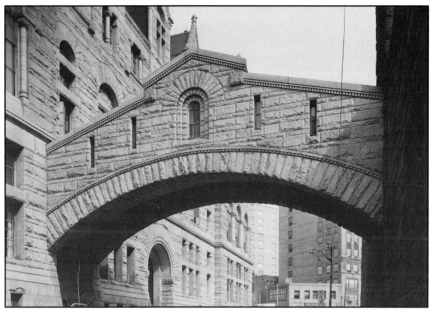

Bridge of Sighs. Courtesy the Library of Congress, Prints and Photographs Division, LOC HABS PA,2-PITBU,29-8.

replaced the canal tunnel and was used to bring mail to the main post office. This same tunnel would eventually be used for the Port Authority's light rail system. But there was an interruption. When the USX tower was built, the tunnel was removed during the deep excavation for the parking garage. During the construction of the garage, the tunnel was reconstructed on a bridge spanning the fourth level of the garage. So the city of Pittsburgh has a bridge (tunnel) inside the USX building carrying light rail traffic.

ALL STEEL SELF-CLEANING BRIDGE

The first all steel self-cleaning bridge in the United States was built over Nine Mile Run near Duck Hollow (McFarren Street) and is still in use today. In 1886 the superstructure of the original bridge at this site was completely replaced with steel girders. The original deck was wood and carried all traffic, including the Braddock trolley line, until 1907. The 1936 Saint Patrick's Day flood washed the wooden deck away leaving the McFarren Street residents virtually isolated. Chief city engineer Henry D. Johnson had the roadway and sidewalk decks replaced with open steel grating, thus creating the first all-steel self-cleaning bridge in America.

The one lane McFarren Avenue Bridge in the Duck Hollow section of the city is the first self-cleaning bridge built in the United States.

Bridge That Is a Landmark

The Panther Hollow Bridge, built in 1897, carries Schenley Drive over Panther Hollow and is a noted landmark in Schenley Park and in the city itself. The bridge is known not for its arch construction but rather for the sculptures of the panthers by Giuseppe Moretti that adorn each corner of the bridge (photos opposite and pages six and 174). Moretti also sculpted the statues of Edward Bigelow across from the nearby Phipps Conservatory, and Stephen Foster located at one entrance to the park near the Carnegie Museum and Library.

Bridge with a Changing Name

While some bridges within the city have names that have changed over the years, there is one nearby whose name changes (or could change) *every* year. The name of the Rochester-Monaca Bridge is determined each year based on the winner of the annual high school football game. This is its current configuration. . . but that could change.

Bridge Names

The Rochester-Monaca Bridge and the various names that Pittsburgh bridges have or had raises the question as to *how* bridges are named. The

The Panther Hollow Bridge in Schenley Park opened in 1897 and was designated a city landmark in 2002.

short answer is that it is a political process. When a bridge is designed or constructed it is given a logical name that is often changed near or upon completion by the political process. One example of this is the road and bridges going up Mount Washington. Originally they were known as the Mount Washington Roadway and Mount Washington Roadway Bridges. However at a later date, the city council with the approval of the mayor changed the name to the P. J. McArdle Roadway and Bridges. A similar process ensues for county bridges, with the county council, and for PennDOT bridges, with the state legislature.

In addition, names were often changed to avoid duplication as surrounding boroughs were annexed by the city.

ABSENCE OF TOLL BRIDGES

It has been noted that Pittsburgh has every type of bridge except a drawbridge. To that we could also add a toll bridge although that was not always the case. Up until the 1890s, all the bridges across the rivers were toll bridges. In 1897 the Point, Smithfield and South 10th Street bridges were purchased by the city and made free. In 1911, the county changed the 6th, 7th, 9th, 16th and 30th Street bridges from toll to free. And the last privately owned toll bridge, the Union Bridge, was replaced by the Manchester, a free bridge, in 1914. In 1915 Brown's Bridge, the predecessor to the Homestead Grays Bridge, and the Highland Park Bridge were made toll-free. The following year, Jack's Run Bridge at the city's limit was made free and the last toll bridge, the Glenwood Bridge, was "freed" in 1926.

Mount Washington Road Bridge tablet at east end of bridge. Courtesy of City of Pittsburgh Department of Public Works, Bureau of Engineering and Construction.

UNDER THE BRIDGES
AND ON THE RIVERS

The Highland Park Bridge spans the Allegheny River connecting the City of Pittsburgh with Aspinwall on the north shore. The Brilliant Branch Railroad Bridge is in the background and the Highland Dam is visible in the foreground.

A bridge, besides providing transportation and connection across an intervening obstacle, also creates a new space *underneath* the structure. While all studies, reports and books on bridges focus on the structures themselves or the traffic they carry, it is also worthwhile to examine the bridge underworld. First of all, a careful examination of these spaces has revealed that all three Billy Goats Gruff could now readily cross any of the city's bridges as there are no trolls beneath them.

40th Street Bridge.

Fort Duquesne Bridge.

The plaques on the abutment wall of the Fort Pitt Boulevard/Parkway East on-ramp (Fort Pitt Bridge) memorialize deceased members of the city's homeless population who lived under the bridges. Inset: *Detail from photo.*

As A Refuge

Anyone who has traversed the lesser-traveled areas under our bridges knows that they are a refuge for many homeless people living in the city. It is inspiring and moving that Project Safety Net, a Mercy Hospital program that provides medical care to this population, chose an area under a bridge to commemorate the deaths of the bridge underworld residents. Memorial plaques, doing so, adorn the abutment wall on Fort Pitt Boulevard of the Parkway East on-ramp from Grant Street.

A Concert Hall

Music can also be heard under the bridges as Rick Sebak reported in his video *Flying Off the Bridge to Nowhere!; and Other Tales of Pittsburgh Bridges.* In this video, he shows Glen Surgest practicing his trumpet under the Fort Duquesne Bridge because of the good acoustics.

The author (2nd from left) joins Officer Nate Hawthorne (left) and paramedics Bill Wilson and Jeff Jones of the River Rescue Unit.

UNDER THE BRIDGES AND ON THE RIVERS

Undoubtedly the most frequent observers of life under the bridges are the members of the City of Pittsburgh's River Rescue Unit. This unit was formed in 1986 by combining the efforts of the Bureau of Emergency Medical Services SCUBA Search and Rescue unit with those of the Police River Patrol. Although their primary mission is to respond to waterborne emergencies within the city, they also conduct routine river patrols during the summer boating season. Each boat is manned by a police officer and two paramedics. The police officers involved in this unit are with the Special Emergency Response Team (SERT) group which was formerly known by the acronym SWAT.

Officer Nate Hawthorne is typical of the police officers assigned to this unit as he served ten years with the Coast Guard before joining the city's police department. He notes that, unfortunately, a lot of their work is rescuing, or recovering the bodies, of those who have jumped from the city bridges. However, they along with the Coast Guard are also responsible for ensuring bridge safety during presidential visits.

We were fortunate to be able to join Officer Hawthorne and paramedics Jeff Jones and Bill Wilson on one of their two hour tours of the city's riverways. It is unfortunate that more city residents don't have such an opportunity to watch these highly trained and dedicated men patrol our waterways. Jones and Wilson are among a group of city paramedics who are divers specially trained for water rescue and recovery. These paramedics work most of the year in the standard paramedic units and rotate into the River Rescue Unit for one to two month periods. Their dive equipment is well suited to the rigors of the rivers as it includes bright underwater lights and special face masks equipped with two-way radio communication.

The River Rescue Unit conducts routine patrols during the boating season conducting boat safety inspections, citing operators under the influence and enforcing the no-wake zone which now extends from the West End Bridge to the Roberto Clemente Bridge on the Allegheny River, and the Smithfield Bridge on the Monongahela River. Since the July 2005 London subway bombings, they (and the Coast Guard) do more frequent river patrols with an eye on the bridges.

Indeed the rivers offer a unique perspective of the bridges. While from a distance they are scenic wonders, from immediately below, like examining the underneath of a car, they appear much more utilitarian. Yet, such a view gives one confidence in their structural integrity. It is also reassuring that along with periodic bridge inspections by bridge owners, there is also a daily (sometimes several times daily) visual inspection of the bridges conducted by the River Rescue Unit and the Coast Guard.

And Hawthorne assures us that unlike Bruce Willis' character in the movie *Striking Distance,* they do not pilot their boats over the area's dams.

Part III
Bridge Tours

The bridges of Pittsburgh are scattered throughout all sections of the city and only ten of the city's ninety neighborhoods are bridge deprived. In order to provide tours for all (or most) of the features that we've written about, we have included suggested tours that can be conducted by car, bicycle, boat or on foot.

There are concessions in downtown Pittsburgh that rent bikes and kayaks. Venture Outdoors (VentureOutdoors.com) is a terrific resource for outdoor activities and vendors.

Happy bridgespotting in whatever way you choose to explore the City of Bridges.

Pittsburgh can be a confusing city to navigate precisely because of the topographic features that make it interesting. Before setting out, get yourself a good street map with a street index to supplement the information that follows. The "cross-hair" on the small locator maps included with longer tours indicate where those tours begin.

Bridges far to near: West End, Fort Pitt, and Smithfield Street.

Incredible views abound from and of the city's bridges. This view of downtown Pittsburgh from the 31st Street Bridge shows the Herr's Island Pedestrian Bridge with downtown in the background.

DRIVING TOUR

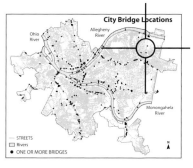

City Bridge Locations

Ohio River

Allegheny River

Monongahela River

STREETS
Rivers
ONE OR MORE BRIDGES

In our daily trips in and about the city we can't avoid encountering bridges of various types and it is hoped that this book can aid in noticing and appreciating these structures. Although a driving tour can start almost anywhere, we chose to start our suggested tour at the *Brilliant Cutoff Viaduct on Washington Boulevard* and end it going over the *Fort Pitt Bridge*. This tour starts at a bridge built in the fashion of the Holy Roman Empire and ends traversing the first bridge designed on a computer.

Start by going northbound on Washington Boulevard. One first encounters the majestic stone multi-arch *Brilliant Cutoff Viaduct* built in 1904 and the adjacent stone arch *Lincoln Avenue Bridge* (1906) after a subtle turn in the road several blocks from the boulevard's intersection with Frankstown Road (1). Continuing down Washington Boulevard you next pass under the *Larimer Avenue Bridge*, a reinforced concrete arch bridge built in 1912 (2).

Highland Drive intersects Washington Boulevard at the traffic light near the Pittsburgh Public Housing Authority Police headquarters. A glance up Highland Drive to the right will reveal another stone arch bridge that is also on the Brilliant Cutoff line (3).

At the end of Washington Boulevard, turn left onto Allegheny River Boulevard and enter the right lane to cross the *Highland Park Bridge* (4). As you cross this 65-year old bridge, you can also view (to the right—5) the 100-year old *Brilliant Branch Railroad Bridge*. The first dam on the Allegheny River is to the left of the bridge although not visible as you cross (6). Once over the bridge, follow the directions to and take Route 28 southbound to the *40th Street Bridge* (8), a distance of about three miles, passing the 62nd Street/Robert D. Fleming Bridge (7) to the left as you travel south.

Crossing the 40th Street Bridge, built in 1924 and also known as *Washington Crossing Bridge*, note the seals of the thirteen original colonies plus that of Allegheny County adorning the railings. The seals are repeated several times as there are a total of 292 cast metal plaques. Once over the bridge turn right onto Butler Street and follow it as it merges into Penn Avenue going toward downtown Pittsburgh (9) (this is Doughboy Square, named for the eponymous statue that you will see

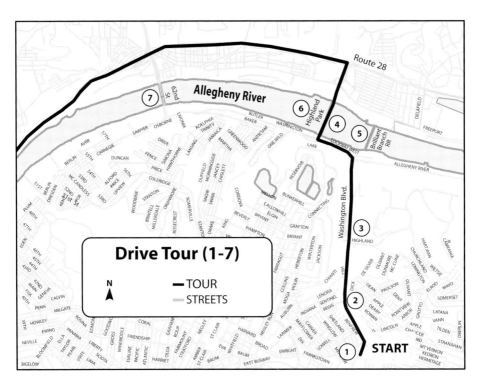

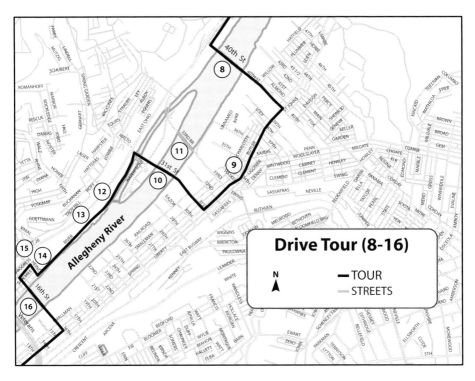

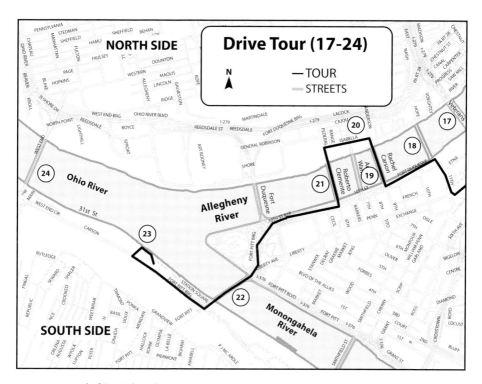

on your left). Take this route to 31st Street and turn right to cross this 76-year old bridge (10).

Note: If the bridge is closed for repair as it's scheduled to be during 2006, continue down Penn Ave to 16th Street and cross the 16th Street Bridge (16). At the end of the bridge turn right onto Progress Street, then right onto Heinz Street, and finally left onto River Avenue. Drive to the parking lot on the left across from the Herr's Island Railroad Bridge (12).

Crossing the *31st Street Bridge*, notice the 33rd St. railroad bridge to the right (11). Turn left onto River Avenue and once down the ramp notice the backchannel railroad bridge (12) that is now part of the city's walking/biking trail system. A small parking lot is on the right side of the road and offers a chance to stop and explore this bridge.

Continue down River Avenue (13) until just past the Heinz plant. Turn right onto Heinz Street (14) and then left on Progress Street (15) (Progress isn't marked from this direction) and finally left on *16th Street* to cross this bridge (16). This spectacular through truss bridge built in 1923 was recently restored to its original grandeur.

After exiting the bridge turn right onto Penn Avenue and after passing under the *Veterans Bridge* (17—1987), turn right onto 11th Street. After passing under the 100-year old *Fort Wayne Railroad Bridge* (18) and the Convention Center, turn left onto Fort Duquesne Boulevard and then right onto the *Rachel Carson Bridge* (19—1927), the first of the Three Sisters. As you cross, note the bicycle chain-like appearance of the supporting eyebar suspension chains.

At the end of the bridge, turn left onto Isabella Street (20). You will cross over Sandusky Street at which point look left and see the bright yellow Andy Warhol Bridge, the middle of the Three Sisters. At the end of Isabella, PNC Park, home of the Pittsburgh Pirates, will be directly in front of you. Turn left onto Federal Street and drive over the Roberto Clemente Bridge (21). Just before you cross the bridge, note the statue of Robert Clemente. And as you cross, note all the bridges that surround you.

Turn right onto Fort Duquesne Boulevard and follow the signs to the *Fort Pitt Bridge* (22) (airport). While crossing this double-decker bridge, stay to the far right and look for an exit to the right that leads to West Carson Street. Taking this exit brings you to West Carson Street and under the Duquesne Incline pedestrian bridge (23). Turn right into the Station Square access road and park in the Duquesne Incline parking lot. As you walk up the stairs, cross the pedestrian bridge to the base of the incline. Take the incline to the top and enjoy the view of the City of Bridges, including the *West End Bridge* (24) on your left.

The Fort Duquesne Bridge is in the background; the truck is on the I-376/Parkway East exit ramp from the Fort Pitt Bridge. The abutment in the left foreground of the photo is from the old Wabash Railroad Bridge.

A COMBINED DRIVING AND WALKING TOUR

The *Wilksboro Avenue and Windgap Suspension Footbridges* are in different parts of the city and definitely worth visiting. We suggest driving to them and then enjoying them on foot.

WILKSBORO AVENUE FOOTBRIDGE

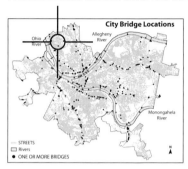

Travel north (outbound) on California Avenue on the city's North Side. At Termon Avenue (1), California turns right and then in a few blocks, it turns left (2). Wilksboro Avenue is the third left (3) off California Avenue after this last change in direction. Turn down the short street to the bridge (4), park and enjoy this most unique feature built in 1895. (See photo on page 93.)

Windgap Suspension Footbridge

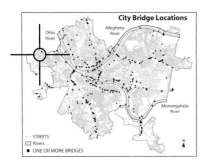

City Bridge Locations

To access the Windgap Suspension Bridge, drive out West Carson Street and turn left into the Corliss Tunnel. Turn right on Chartiers Avenue and follow it almost to the end where it intersects with Windgap Avenue at a traffic light (1). Turn right on Windgap Avenue and then take the third right off Windgap Avenue (2—Youghiogheny Street) just before the Windgap Avenue Bridge. The first left off this street (3—Township Road) leads to the bridge. Park at the turn in the road (4) and explore the Windgap Suspension Bridge (5). Located here at the city limit are a railroad, vehicle, and pedestrian bridge providing all types of transport access to the city. (See photo on page 94.)

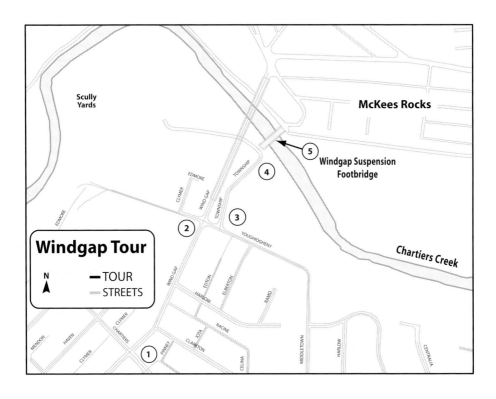

WALKING TOURS

I. Downtown Walk Through History

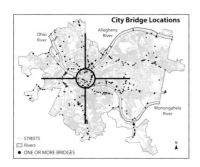

Start near the Hilton Hotel (1) across from Point State Park. From the front of the hotel, turn right and walk down Commonwealth Place to Fort Duquesne Boulevard (2). Turn right again and walk to the *Roberto Clemente Bridge* (3—1928). Walking across this bridge is the best way to see it. Indeed this is probably the most walked bridge in the city as it is closed for Pirates home games and used solely

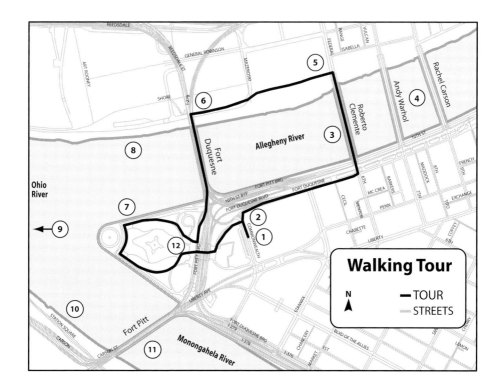

as a pedestrian bridge. As you cross, notice the structure of the bridge and the new lighting that has been added. Also stop and look upstream at the other Three Sisters and bridges beyond (4).

Once over the bridge walk through PNC Park on the left (5) (the back gates are open on non-game days allowing passage along the riverside to Mazeroski Way). Then walk down North Shore Drive toward Heinz Field to the access ramp for the *Fort Duquesne Bridge* (6) pedestrian ramp. (Before you head up the pedestrian ramp, follow the walkway down to the river for a plaque commemorating the site of the first World Series played at Exposition Park which was located in this area.) As you cross the Fort Duquesne Bridge (1963), realize that it is rare to have a pedestrian walkway on an interstate highway bridge and enjoy the view.

Once in Point State Park, turn to the right down toward the water and then turn left along the path to the fountain at the Point where the Allegheny and Monongahela rivers join to form the Ohio River (7). From here, you can look towards Heinz Field and see the pier (8) that once supported the Manchester Bridge (1915). This bridge and its predecessor the Union Bridge (1875) spanned the Allegheny from this spot on the Point to the area where Heinz Field is now located. Looking straight down the Ohio you can see the *West End Bridge* (9). This through truss bridge was built in 1932 and has been recently rehabilitated. Looking to the left, note a pier (10) at the other side of the Monongahela River that once supported one of the Point bridges that spanned this river.

Walking along the banks of the Monongahela, you come to the *Fort Pitt Bridge* (11—1959), the double-decker bridge that replaced the earlier Point Bridges. To exit the park and return to the area of the Hilton Hotel, pass *over* a footbridge *under* the *Portal Bridge* (12—1963). Stop and note the beauty of the Portal Bridge that supports an interstate highway.

Pedestrians crossing the Roberto Clemente Bridge on their way to PNC Park.

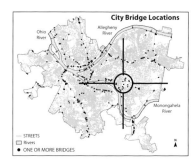

City Bridge Locations

II. SCHENLEY PARK

The Schenley Park Visitors Center (1) located on Panther Hollow Road across from the Phipps Conservatory (2), offers a good place to start. Colorful detailed maps of the park showing the trails and locations of all the bridges are available at the center, but in case they are closed at the time of your tour, we've included an abbreviated version below. Note that the names are not well marked along the trail, but it's easy to find your way.

Behind the center travel down the steps and trail until the main trail (Lower Panther Hollow Bridle Trail) at the bottom and then turn left. Almost immediately you will cross a *tufa bridge* on the trail (3). Continue along until you notice another trail (4—Lake Trail) going down to the right leading to Panther Hollow Lake (5). Take this trail and notice the various WPA bridges and one tufa bridge no longer in use that adorn a previous trail.

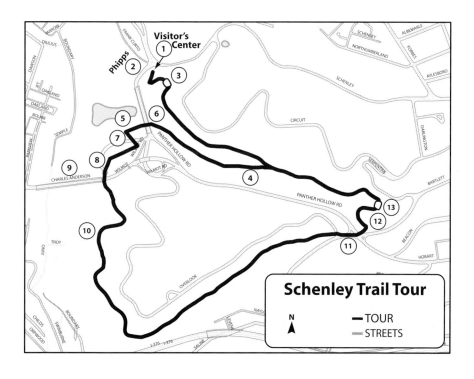

Schenley Trail Tour

Once under the 1897 Panther Hollow Bridge (6) walk along the left side of the lake. You will notice a flight of steps on the left (7). Take these up to the upper trail (8) which travels not only under the Panther Hollow Bridge (1897) but also under the 1940 Charles Anderson Bridge (9). Turn right at the top of the steps and continue on the upper trail to reach the Anderson Bridge. Once under the Anderson Bridge, bear left through a public works storage area to reach the Locust Trail (10). Turn right on the Locust Trail to cross over several WPA bridges and to its end at the intersection of Greenfield Avenue, Panther Hollow, and Bartlett Street (11). Cross Panther Hollow Road and take the trail beside the Bartlett Street Playground staying to the right (12). This is once again the lower Panther Hollow Trail. After crossing one of the largest tufa bridges (13), it leads back to the visitors center (1).

Lake in Panther Hollow. Schenley Park, Pittsburg. Pa. By Night.

This turn of the century postcard gave a romantic view of Schenley Park's Panther Hollow Bridge in the early days of the twentieth century. There are plans to restore the lake; the boathouse is no longer there. Courtesy of the Pittsburgh Parks Conservancy.

BICYCLE TOURS

I. Tour du Ponts-Sud (southern tour of the bridges)

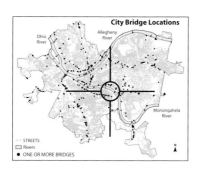

City Bridge Locations

Ohio River
Allegheny River
Monongahela River

STREETS
Rivers
ONE OR MORE BRIDGES

The parking lot off Second Avenue at the end of the Eliza Furnace Trail at Swinburne Street and Second Avenue (1) serves as a good starting point for this tour. Start by riding down the access road (Swinburne Street) to Second Avenue passing under two former railroad bridges that are now part of the bike trail. Turn right onto Second Avenue and you will soon pass under a pedestrian bridge that carries a set of city steps safely over the road (2). At the second set of traffic lights turn left onto the *Monongahela Connecting Bridge* (3—1904) and as you bike over the bridge note the similarities in the structure between this bridge and the adjacent and four year older *Hot Metal Bridge* (4). At the end turn left onto the paved bike trail and leisurely travel it to its end enjoying river views and views of the *Glenwood* (1966) and *Glenwood B&O Railroad* (1915) *Bridges* (5) as you do so. It's a dead end trail so turn at the end and head back toward Pittsburgh.

Becks Run Road is off to your left at about the mid-point of the trail. Notice the *railroad bridge* (6) over this road that is complete with unplanned-for foliage growing on its deck. As you continue on the trail notice across East Carson Street the various structures that transport the railroad. Stop off the trail at the Steelers training facility (7) and enjoy the view (from the outside) of the mural over the cafeteria area.

Continue on the trail past Hot Metal Street until its end at South 4th Street. Along this stretch you will notice the railroad disappears into a tunnel before Hot Metal Street to reemerge again near the end of South 25th Street, the *Birmingham Bridge* (8—1977) and finally the only true wire suspension bridge in the city—the *South 10th Street Bridge* (9—1931).

At the end of the trail turn left onto South 4th Street (10) and ride to McKean Street and then turn right (11). Travel on this street under the *Liberty Bridge* (12) until just past the Allegheny County vehicle garage and turn right on South 2nd Street (13) to access the end of the bicycle trail again (14). Take this toward Station Square traveling under the

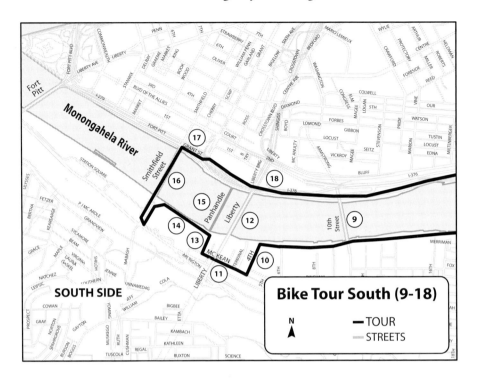

The Glenwood Bridge with its Warren Truss construction is easily visible from the Trail when you take the southern bike tour. You may even spot a series of barges moving their massive loads. The Glenwood B&O Railroad Bridge is in the background.

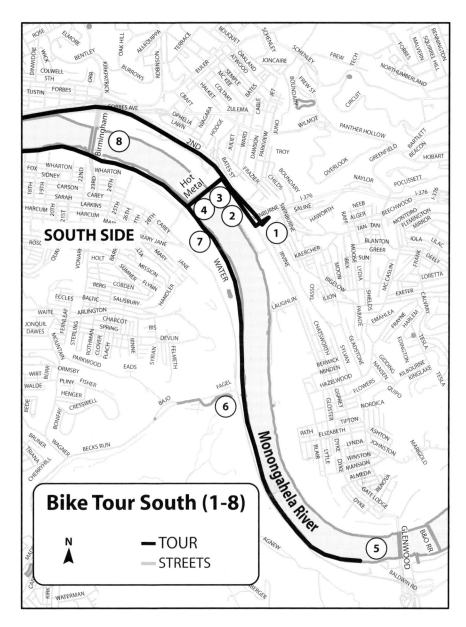

Panhandle Bridge (15—1904). Next to the trail under the Panhandle Bridge are several derelict railroad cars, one of which (and it's obvious which one) is a torpedo car that was used to carry hot metal over the Hot Metal Bridge.

Exit the path before Station Square and work your way to the *Smithfield Street Bridge* (1883), the oldest bridge in the city (16). Travel

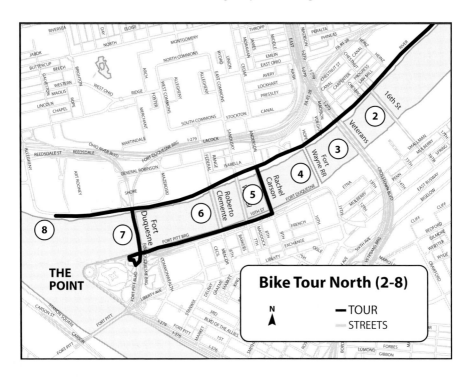

across this lenticular through-truss bridge and turn right onto the Boulevard of the Allies (17); proceed to the traffic lights at the intersection with Grant Street. *Carefully* cross Grant Street to the start of the Eliza Furnace Trail at the PNC Bank building (18). Take the trail back to the start of the Tour and notice a different view of the bridges that were observed in the earlier part of the ride on the south side of the river.

II. TOUR DU PONTS-NORD (NORTHERN TOUR OF THE BRIDGES)

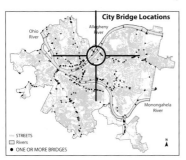

This tour starts in the small parking lot off River Avenue opposite the *Three Rivers Heritage Trail Railroad Bridge* (1) on the north side of the Allegheny River. Travel over this bridge to explore Washington's Landing (Herr's Island), and the various bridges around it and then return to the river trail heading toward downtown Pittsburgh. Riding this path you travel under the *16th Street* (2—1923), the *Veterans* (3—1987), and the *Fort Wayne Railroad* (4—1904) *Bridges*. Once past these

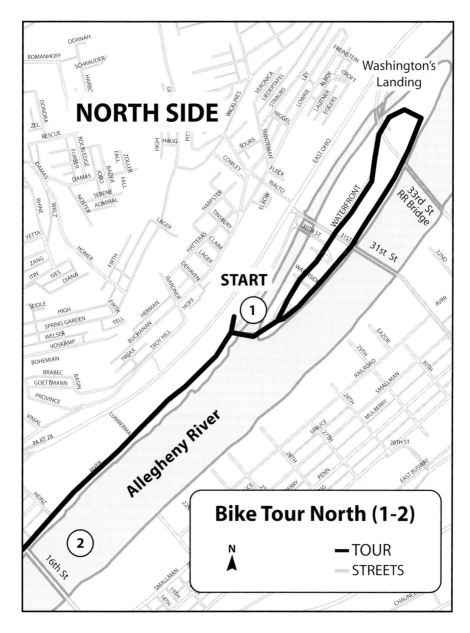

ride up to 9th Street and cross the first of the Three Sisters (5), the *Rachel Carson*. After you cross the bridge ride down to the path along the other side of the river and travel under the *other Sisters* (6) and the *Fort Duquesne Bridge* (7). Bicycles are not allowed in Point State Park but it is okay to ride up the paths (on the left) to the access ramp to the *Fort Duquesne Bridge* (1963). Travel this pedestrian walkway *slowly* and stop occasionally to notice the view downstream, including the Manchester Bridge (1915) pier near Heinz Field and the *West End Bridge* (1932). At the northern end of the bridge turn left and ride to the *Manchester Bridge pier* (8) where you can once again access the bike trail. Riding back to the starting point provides another view of all the major Allegheny River bridges.

Walking or biking gives you a chance to examine the details on the bridges. This is the 16th Street Bridge visible on the northern bike tour.

RIVER TOURS

In discussing bridges, the rivers are seen as impediments or obstacles to be overcome. In fact they are one of the city's greatest assets, without which the city would not have occurred. The rivers also offer an opportunity to obtain unique views of the city's most famous bridges. Indeed a river cruise of these structures is a highlight of the annual International Bridge Conference every June.

Although there is no truth to the urban myth that Allegheny County has the second highest number of registered boats in the U.S. after Dade County, Florida, there are a great number of pleasure boats in the county (approximately 30,000). This is only one indication of the potential traffic on the rivers, and one option for touring the bridges. In addition there are tour boats and unregistered pleasure craft such as kayaks and canoes.

One interesting tour of the bridges on the Allegheny River is offered by the Lawrenceville Historical Society in their annual Rolling on the Allegheny River Tour. This tour on the Pittsburgh Voyager offers informative historical insights into the areas of the city along the Allegheny River.

The author's three year old grandson pilots a "Ducky" boat on the Ohio River; the Fort Duquesne Bridge is visible in the background. Photo by Meg Regan Wingard.

A River Rescue boat's eye view of the 16th Street Bridge in the background.

As there are not set paths to be taken in the waterways it is difficult to dictate a prescribed path for a river tour of the city's bridges. However, as an aid we offer bridge descriptions for three areas of the rivers: downtown excursion, the upper Mon and the upper Al. It should be noted that all the city bridges with the exception of the Highland Park Bridge are within the Emsworth Dam Pool and can be visited without traversing a lock.

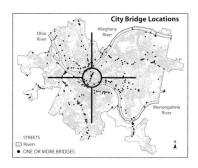

DOWNTOWN EXCURSION

The many downtown bridges are routinely visited by many boat cruises and can even be appreciated when traveling by boat to a football or baseball game. We start at the *South 10th Street Bridge* on the Mon (1) and then traverse to the *16th Street Bridge* (11) on the Beautiful River (original name of the Allegheny).

The *South 10th Street Bridge* (1), the longest bridge on the Monongahela River and the only true suspension bridge in the city,

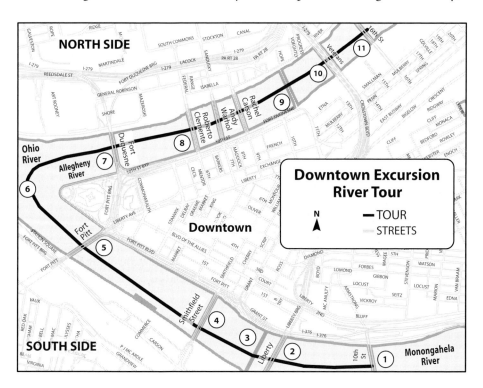

was built by Allegheny County in 1931. Traveling downstream the next bridge is the *Liberty Bridge (2)* and the *Panhandle Bridge* (3) whose proper name is the Monongahela River Bridge and the only river crossing light rail bridge in the city. It was built in 1904.

Continue down the river to encounter the oldest bridge in the city—the *Smithfield Street Bridge* (4) built by Gustav Lindenthal in 1883. This was also the site of the first river crossing bridge in the city. The stone piers on either side of the river past the Smithfield Street Bridge are remnants of the Wabash Railroad Bridge. This bridge was built in 1904 and carried trains from downtown to the Wabash Tunnel. It was dismantled in 1948 and its components recycled into the Dravosburg Bridge which also spans the Monongahela River. It is only a short distance from the remnants of the Wabash Bridge, built in a cantilever style, to the modern two-deck *Fort Pitt Bridge* (5—1959) which was designed on a computer. Just past the Fort Pitt Bridge on the southern banks of the river is another stone pier. This is all that is left of the second bridge spanning the Monongahela River at the Point known simply as Point Bridge #2.

Briefly visiting the waters of the Ohio River while circling the Point note off in the distance the *West End Bridge* (6), built by Allegheny County in 1932. Also note the stone pier by Heinz Field. This was part of the Manchester Bridge (1915), the second bridge at this site. Starting up the Allegheny the first bridge encountered is the infamous Bridge to Nowhere, also known as the *Fort Duquesne Bridge* (7). It was recently repainted; this double-decker bridge is 46 feet above the river level.

Past the Fort Duquesne Bridge are the *Three Sisters Bridges* (8—Roberto Clemente, Andy Warhol and Rachel Carson) and one can revel in encountering the only three identical side-by-side bridges in the world. Although they resemble suspension bridges, they are rather self-anchored suspension bridges and were built in the late 1920s.

Continuing up the river the next bridge is the dramatic *Fort Wayne Railroad Bridge* (9), another double-decker bridge, but this one for railroads and built in 1904. Immediately past this bridge and in sharp contrast is the rather utilitarian *Veterans Bridge* (10) built in 1987. The last bridge on this tour is the *16th Street Bridge* (11) originally built in 1923, recently restored to its original beauty, and a fitting last bridge to visit on this tour.

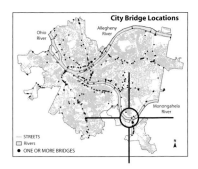

City Bridge Locations

THE UPPER MON RIVER TOUR

Starting above the *South 10th Street Bridge* (1) and heading upstream the first bridge is the *Birmingham Bridge* (2) built in 1977 to replace the original Brady or South 22nd Street Bridge. Next is the "two-in-one" bridge, i.e., the *Hot Metal* (1900) and the *Monongahela Connecting Railroad* (1904) (3). Note the similarity between these two structures. Continuing on the next bridge is the *Glenwood Bridge* (4). This unusual through truss bridge was built in 1966 and refurbished in 2000. Just past this is the *Glenwood B&O Railroad Bridge* (5) that dates to 1915. The last bridge over the river within the city is the *Homestead Grays Bridge* (6), a 68-year old bridge undergoing major renovations and repairs that started in early 2006.

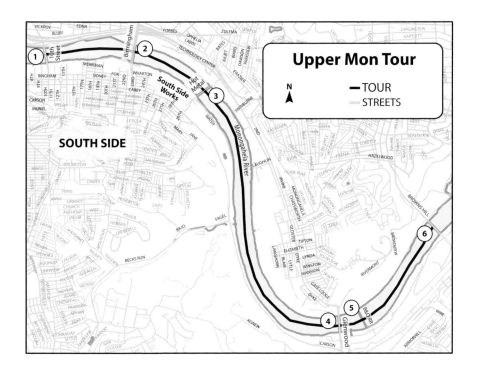

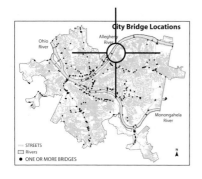

The Upper Al River Tour

Starting above the *16th Street Bridge* (1) the next suite of bridges is those around or connected to Washington Landing (Herr's Island). The *backchannel railroad bridge* (2) is now a part of the city's walking/biking trail system. The first bridge over the Allegheny River is the *31st Street Bridge* (3) and this 76-year old bridge is due for rehabilitation during 2006. The next bridge is the *33rd Street Railroad Bridge* (4) built in the early 1920s. Two more bridges cross the Allegheny before the lock. These are the *40th Street (Washington Crossing) Bridge* (5) (1924) and the *62nd Street (R.D. Fleming) Bridge* (6) (1962).

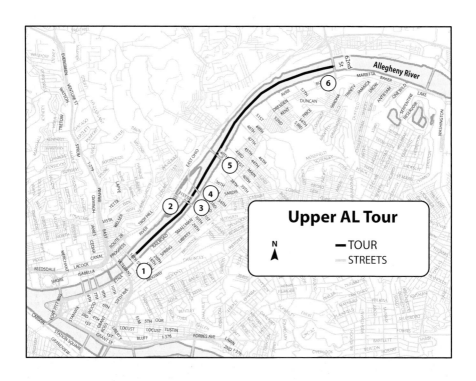

Opposite: *The Birmingham Bridge with the South Side Slopes in the background.*

EPILOGUE

THE FUTURE

The Smithfield Street Bridge won designation by the Association for Bridge Construction and Design in 1995 as the outstanding rehabilitative bridge.

The many older dates associated with the various bridges throughout the city may lead one to think that bridge building in the 'burgh is a thing of the past. This is far from true as plans by the various entities that own the bridges in the city can readily attest.

At the beginning of 2006, Allegheny County had 32 bridge design projects underway. These included plans for new and replacement bridges. It is interesting to look at the funding sources for these projects. Four projects are funded under a federal program in which the federal government pays 80%, the state 15%, and the county 5% of the cost. Twenty-two are state funded projects, wherein the state government pays most of the cost; the remaining six projects are funded entirely by the citizens of Allegheny County.

Another aspect of these various types of programs is that approval for federally funded projects takes about five years, for state projects three to four years, while sole county projects can be almost immediately approved. Probably the project with the biggest impact on local travel will be the $30 million state-funded rehabilitation of the 68-year-old Homestead Grays Bridge.

The City of Pittsburgh also has an active bridge program planned. Although their only construction project for the year 2006 is the South Millvale Avenue Bridge, there are several bridge replacement projects in the design phase. These include the rehabilitation of the P. J. McArdle Roadway Viaduct #1 (the rehabilitation of Viaduct #2 was completed in 2004), the Fancourt Street, South Highland Avenue, Carnahan Road and Bates Street bridges. The Ridge Avenue Bridge, now closed, will be demolished and unfortunately for some, there are no plans to rehabilitate or replace the Davis Avenue Bridge.

In addition to the footbridges across the East Busway, another new pedestrian bridge will soon be joining the catalogue of footbridges within the city. The Hot Metal Bridge will be designed to take pedestrians and cyclists from the Eliza Furnace Trail (a/k/a the "Jail Trial") on the north side of the Monongahela River to the trails and South Side Works development on the south side of the river.

PennDOT has an aggressive bridge and road program planned throughout Southwestern Pennsylvania. Of interest and impact to the residents of the city is the $21 million rehabilitation of the 31st Street Bridge and the replacement of the load-limited Boulevard of the Allies Bridge (actually two of them) over Forbes Avenue. In keeping with the concern about the aesthetics of our bridges, this replacement has been designed to serve as an attractive and suitable gateway to Oakland. Associated with the replacement bridge(s) will be construction of a new approach ramp to the westbound Boulevard of the Allies from Fifth Avenue negating the existing awkward turns onto Craft Avenue and Forbes Avenue.

The Port Authority plans include only negative bridges (tunnels) but they are spectacular. During 2006, the Port Authority plans to start boring twin tunnels under the Allegheny River to provide light rail service to the North Side.

So, the future of Pittsburgh bridges is bright and healthy. It should also be noted that the city is still at the forefront of bridge building technology as the newer bridges are even better built than those in the past. An example of this is the Port Authority's new Corliss Flyover Bridge

Fireworks at the Point.

providing bus access from West Carson Street to the West Busway. The bridge is constructed of weathering steel and the deck and interior sides are coated with a material to resist penetration by water and salt. It goes without saying that it is also a very visually appealing structure.

Another new Port Authority bridge, connecting to the Wasbash Tunnel, is similarly constructed. In addition, the bridge exterior has an anti-graffiti coating.

LIGHT 'EM UP

The bridges would benefit by lighting them in a dramatic fashion for "Light Up" night, the kick-off of the holiday shopping season, and in a more modest fashion on a permanent basis. The permanent lighting of the Roberto Clemente Bridge shows that such an approach can highlight a bridge in an attractive manner.

A December, 4, 2001 editorial in the *Pittsburgh Post-Gazette* best makes a case for the lighting of the bridges and for their importance to the City of Pittsburgh:

In 1929, on the 50th anniversary of the light bulb, Duquesne Light Co. illuminated bridges here. In 1990, the old Greater Pittsburgh Office of Promotion conducted a bridge lighting demonstration project on parts of the Fort Duquesne Bridge and of the Sixth Street Bridge, now known as the Roberto Clemente Bridge. Four years ago city Councilman Sala Udin called on local corporations to pay for lighting 12 city bridges. . . Each has a story; each has interesting features and details that could be highlighted by illumination and be a source of pride for the region.

The Herr's Island Bridge

By David A. Tolge
Christ the Divine Teacher Catholic
Academy 2005

The Herr's Island Bridge was built in 1890 and rebuilt in 1903. It is also called the West Penn Railroad Bridge and the South Railroad Bridge. It is now part of the Three Rivers Heritage Trail. At 150 feet total length, the design is Platt-Truss. The Herr's Island Bridge has been used for many things. While researching, I found this interesting article in the Science and Technology Room of the Oakland Branch of the Andrew Carnegie Library.

Pittsburgh Sun-Telegraph
Monday, April 24, 1939

Old Herr's Island Bridge Wrecked

The rescue of a pigeon featured the demolition today of the old Herr's Island Bridge across the back channel of the Allegheny River. The bridge was replaced two weeks ago by a modern span, the first in the city's $15,000,000 improvement program. As the 30 year old mass of steel and iron went hurtling into the Allegheny River, a pigeon's nest fell with it. The mother pigeon was sitting on a nest of eggs. Workman put out from the bank in a rowboat and rescued the mother bird, but failed to find the nest. The mother suffered a broken wing.

Herr's Island Bridge

I also found newspaper articles about why the bridge was rebuilt. The old Herr's Island Bridge was physically unstable and the actual reason that they made a new one is because of an accident that occurred on January 18, 1924 at 10:45 a.m. John T. Richards was helping to bring a truckload of pigs to the Herr's Island slaughtering plant when a beam fell causing the truck to fall into the river. Mr. Richards drowned but the driver of the truck lived by hanging onto a pig's tail while it swam to shore. Later in court, the City of Pittsburgh was blamed for not fixing the bridge, knowing that it was a hazard before the accident. ("Jury Blames City for Fatal Bridge Crash", *Gazette-Times* February 9, 1926)

I started to build my bridge model with the help of my parents who bought the supplies and glued the wood sticks that I couldn't handle on my own. First, we needed to figure out how to model it. Then we visited the real bridge. I looked carefully at the structure for anything that I didn't see in a picture that I had of the Herr's Island Bridge. While there, I found that at both end of the bridge, one side was longer than the other and the crossbeams on each side were unequal.*

Later, after writing down my findings, I made a model with unequal crossbeams and sides. I built crossbeams for the top and bottom of the model. Finally, I used a piece of plywood, painted a river on it with crayon and marker, nailed down small cuts of wood for bridge supports, and lastly, glued all the main pieces together to complete the Herr's Island Bridge.

In the Science and Technology Room in the Oakland Branch of the Carnegie Library, my dad and I met a professor from the University of Pittsburgh. We were busy looking through information about the Herr's Island Bridge when we met Professor Regan. He was waiting to look at the folder of old newspaper articles about Pittsburgh's bridges that we were reading. We said hello and talked about the fourth grade bridge report that I was doing. Mr. Regan told us that he was writing a book about all of the bridge of Pittsburgh and he was interested in our social studies class project. My dad asked my teacher, Mrs. Casile, and

Mr. Marino, the principal, if it would be okay for Mr. Regan to come to school and talk about his book. Mr. Marino said yes, so Mr. Regan visited the fourth grade to look at everyone's bridge model. He talked about his book about the bridges of Pittsburgh and answered a lot of questions from my class.

Bibliography:

Gangewere, Robert J. *The Bridges of Pittsburgh and Allegheny County*. Science and Technology Department, Carnegie Library of Pittsburgh, 2001.

"The Bridge Crash Horror". *Gazette-Times*, January 21, 1924.

"Jury Blames City for Fatal Bridge Crash". *Gazette-Times*, February 9, 1926.

"Herr's Island Span to Roll into Traffic Service Today". *Pittsburgh Press*, April 9, 1939.

"Old Herr's island Bridge Wrecked". *Pittsburgh Sun-Telegraph*, April 24, 1939.

www.pghbridges.com, a Web site produced and maintained by Bruce S. Cridlebaugh ("Just a way to satisfy my curiosity and share the results with others...").

* *Bob Regan explains that trains had to make a sharp turn to get onto the bridge resulting in the uneven crossbeam design.*

This article was written as part of a 4th grade class project by David A. Tolge, Christ the Divine Teacher Catholic Academy, Aspinwall, PA.

APPENDIX II: THE BIG LIST

Number of Pittsburgh Bridges	
Owned and Maintained by	Bridges
Allegheny County	21
City of Pittsburgh	126
PennDOT	186
Port Authority	42
Railroads	71
Total	**446**

Bridges within or at the boundary of the City of Pittsburgh

Owned and Maintained by Allegheny County	
Bridge	Location/Description
Andy Warhol (7th Street)	Allegheny River, Downtown
Becks Run Road (#1)	Becks Run
Becks Run Road (#2)	Becks Run
Becks Run Road (#3)	Becks Run
Becks Run Road (#4)	Becks Run
Becks Run Road (#5)	Becks Run
Becks Run Road (#6)	Becks Run
Becks Run Road (#7)	Becks Run
California Avenue	Belgium Street
Colerain Street	Near Saw Mill Run Blvd.
Glenwood Bridge	Monongahela River
Homestead Grays (High Level)	Monongahela River
Ivory Avenue	McKnight Road
Oakwood Road	Pennsdale Street
Rachel Carson (9th Street)	Allegheny River, Downtown
Ramp Street	Baldwin Road/Mifflin Road
Roberto Clemente (6th Street)	Allegheny River, Downtown
16th Street	Monongahela River
10th Street	Monongahela River
Township Road	Chartiers Creek
Windgap Avenue	Chartiers Creek
Total Owned and Maintained by Allegheny County: 21	

City of Pittsburgh's Bureau of Bridges Pierce Arrow truck, 1926. Courtesy of City of Pittsburgh Department of Public Works, Bureau of Engineering and Construction.

Owned and Maintained by the City of Pittsburgh	
Bridge	Location/Description
Alexander Street	Saw Mill Creek
Allegheny Park (footbridge)	Allegheny Park
Anderson, Chas. Memorial	Blvd. of Allies/Four Mile Run
Ansonia Place	Saw Mill Creek
Arcata Way	Arcata at Fairhaven
Bajo Street	Becks Run
Baldwick Road (#1)	Baldwick Road
Baldwick Road (#2)	Baldwick Road
Baldwick Road (#3)	Baldwick Road
Baum Boulevard	Baum Blvd. at Neville
Bloomfield	Bloomfield Bridge
Boehm Street Footbridge	I-376
Broome Street Footbridge	Baldwin Road
Calera Street (#1)	Streets Run
Calera Street (#2)	Streets Run
Carnahan Road	At Banksville Road

Owned and Maintained by the City of Pittsburgh	
Bridge	Location/Description
Carson Street West	At Steuben Street
Chartiers Avenue	West Busway
Chartiers Creek (#1)	Near Stanhope Street
Chestnut Street	Route 28 Ramps
Columbus Avenue	At California Avenue
Commercial Street	Nine Mile Run
Crane Avenue	Saw Mill Run
Davis Avenue	Woods Run Avenue
Eads Street	At Parkwood Road
East Liberty Boulevard—North	Near Negley Run Blvd.
East Liberty Boulevard—South	Near Negley Run Blvd.
Edgebrook Avenue	Saw Mill Run
E. H. Swindell	Over I-279
Eliza Furnace Trail (#1)	Second Avenue
Eliza Furnace Trail (#2)	Pedestrian Overpass
Eliza Furnace Trail (#3)	Bates Street
Eliza Furnace Trail (#4)	Pedestrian Overpass
Eliza Furnace Trail (#5)	Swinburne Street
Eliza Furnace Trail #6	Swinburne Street
Elizabeth Street	Gloster Street
Englert Street Footbridge	Saw Mill Run
Fairhaven Road	At Saw Mill Run
Fancourt Street	Fort Dusquesne On-Ramp
Finland Street	Bigelow Blvd.
Forbes Avenue (#1)	Boundary Street
Forbes Avenue (#2)	Frick Park
Fort Pitt Boulevard	Near Commonwealth Place
Franum Street	Saw Mill Run
Fritz Street	Near Welsh Way
Ganges Way	At Railside Street
Goettman Street	Goettman Street
Greenfield Avenue	I-376
Herron Avenue	East Busway
Herr's Island	Second Avenue
Hill Road	Pittsburgh Zoo

Owned and Maintained by the City of Pittsburgh	
Bridge	Location/Description
Hillview Road	Saw Mill Run
Hot Metal	Hot Metal Bridge
Howard Street	I-279
Larimer Avenue (#1)	Washington Blvd.
Larimer Avenue (#2)	Brilliant Branch RR
Lincoln Avenue	Washington Blvd.
Lowe Street	Near Woodville Avenue
Lowrie Street	Rialto
Maple Avenue	Charles Street
Market Street	I-376
Meadow Street	Negley Run Blvd
Melanchton Street Footbridge	Near Second Avenue
Midwood Street Footbridge	Saw Mill Run
Milroy Street	I-279
Mission Street East	Quarry Street
Mission Street West	VonArk Street
Moredale Street Footbridge	South Busway
Monongahela Connecting Railroad	Hot Metal Street
Murray Avenue	Beechwood Blvd.
North Avenue & Brighton Road	North Avenue and Brighton Road
North Avenue	I-279
North Lang Street Footbridge	East Busway
Ohio River Blvd (#1)	Eckert Street
Ohio River Blvd (#2)	Near McKees Rocks Bridge
One Wild Place	Pittsburgh Zoo
Overbrook Way Footbridge	Saw Mill Run
Penn Avenue	East Busway
Pennsdale (#1)	Pennsdale Street
Pennsdale (#2)	Pennsdale Street
Pennsylvania Avenue	Railroad
P. J. McArdle Roadway (#1)	Near Sycamore Street
P. J. McArdle Roadway (#2)	Near Grandview Avenue
P. J. McArdle Viaduct (#1)	7th Street
P. J. McArdle Viaduct (#2)	Near Arlington Avenue
Plank Street	Wabash Street/Independence Way

Owned and Maintained by the City of Pittsburgh	
Bridge	Location/Description
Radcliffe Street	Near Stadium Street
Ramp Q	I-279
Rankin Avenue Footbridge	Ohio River Blvd.
Ridge Avenue	Railroad
River Avenue Viaduct	Railroad
Robert McAfee	California Avenue/Eckert Street
Schenley Park	Schenley Park
Schenley Park (Locust Trail #1)	Schenley Park
Schenley Park (Locust Trail #2)	Schenley Park
Schenley Park (Panther Hollow)	Schenley Park
Schenley Park (Trail #1)	Schenley Park
Schenley Park (Trail #2)	Schenley Park
Schenley Park (Trail #3)	Schenley Park
Schenley Park (Trail #4)	Schenley Park
Schenley Park (Underpass)	Schenley Park
Second Avenue	Footbridge
Service Road	I-279
Shadeland Avenue	Woods Run Avenue
Shaler Street	Saw Mill Run
South Aiken Avenue	East Busway
South 15th Street	Footbridge
South Graham Street Footbridge	East Busway
South Highland Avenue	East Busway
South Millvale Avenue	East Busway
South Negley Avenue	East Busway
South 10th Street	Footbridge
South 12th Street	Railroad
Stanwix Street	I-376
Swinburne Street (Frazier)	Four Mile Run
Sycamore Street	Sycamore Street
Termon Avenue	Verner Avenue
Timberland Avenue	Saw Mill Run
Tripoli Street	I-279
Troy Hill Road	Hillside
28th Street	East Busway

Owned and Maintained by the City of Pittsburgh	
Bridge	Location/Description
Unnamed Way Footbridge	Streets Run
Warrington Avenue	Near Boggstown Avenue
Western Avenue	Railroad
Wilksboro Avenue Footbridge	Near California Avenue
Wood Street	I-376
Total Owned and Maintained by the City of Pittsburgh: 126	

The 62nd Street Bridge (1962) is more formally known as the R. D. Fleming Bridge. It is owned and maintained by PennDOT.

Key for list (starting on the next page) of bridges owned and maintained by PennDOT.

SR	State Route
TR	Truck Route
LR	Legislative Route
NB	North Bound
SB	South Bound
EB	East Bound
WB	West Bound
HOV	High Occupancy Vehicle lanes

Owned and Maintained by PennDOT	
Bridge	Location/Description
1021 HOV 22+52	HOV from Heinz Field
1039 NB	Approach to Fort Duquesne
141-Ramp to Blvd./A	Pittsburgh over Maurice Way
142-Ramp from Blvd./A	LR 120 over Forbes Avenue
376 Eastbound	I-376 EB over Mon Wharf
Allegheny River Blvd.	Pittsburgh–Penn Hills Line
Allegheny River Blvd.	1 1/2 miles east of PA 8
Banksville Road	Near Carnahan Road
Banksville Road	Near Carnahan Road
Banksville Road	Under 19 SB near Crane Avenue
Banksville Road	Near Parkway Interchange
Banksville Road	Near Runaway Truck Ramp
Banksville Road	Pittsburgh
Baum Blvd.	1 mile south of Bloomfield Bridge
Bedford Avenue	Bedford Avenue over 228, 1026
Bigelow Blvd.	Bigelow Blvd. WB over I-579
Bigelow Blvd.	TR 380 WB over 7th Avenue
Bigelow Blvd.	At Herron Avenue
Birmingham Bridge	Birmingham Bridge
Birmingham Bridge	Birmingham Bridge Approach
Blvd. of the Allies	Blvd. of the Allies over Forbes Avenue
Blvd. of the Allies	Brady Street Interchange
Blvd. of the Allies	At Stevenson Street
Blvd. of the Allies	Allies Ramp to Liberty Bridge
Butler Street	Heath's Run Bridge near Zoo
California Avenue	California Avenue over TR 65
Centre Avenue	Centre Avenue over 1026
Chartiers Avenue	McKees Rocks over River
Cross Street	West End Circle
Crosstown Blvd.	1026 NB over 5th Avenue
Crosstown Blvd.	1026 SB over 5th Avenue
Crosstown Blvd.	1026 SB over Ramp D
Crosstown Blvd.	HOV South approach to Veterans Bridge
Crosstown Blvd.	SB I-579 to Liberty Bridge
Crosstown Blvd.	Ramp from Blvd. to 1026 NB
Crosstown Ramp K	Ramp K EB over Ramp B NB

Owned and Maintained by PennDOT	
Bridge	Location/Description
East Ohio Street	East Ohio Street under SR 0579
East Street Valley Extension	I-279 over Suffolk Street
Eighth Avenue	West Homestead-Pittsburgh Line
Fort Duquesne Bridge	I-279 NB-SB Fort Duquesne Bridge
Fort Pitt Bridge	Fort Pitt Bridge Upper Deck
Fort Pitt Bridge	Fort Pitt Bridge over Mon River
Fortieth Street Bridge	40th Street Bridge over Allegheny River
Glass Run Road	1 1/2 miles from Glenwood Interchange
Glass Run Road	Near SR 3100
Glass Run Road	Near Glenwood Interchange
I-279 Ramp F	LR 1039 lower approach Fort Duquesne
I-279 SB	279 SB over SRs 4003 and 4009
Interstate 579	North end of Veterans Bridge
Lebanon Road	At intersection SR 2045
Lebanon Road	At intersection SR 2045
Lebanon Road	350 feet northwest of intersection SR 2045
Lebanon Road	1/2 miles northwest of SR 2045
Lebanon Road	200 feet north of Glass Run Road
Liberty Bridge	Liberty Bridge
Library Road	300 feet northeast of McNeilly Road
Library Road	Pittsburgh at 51 and 88
LR 1039, Sta. 976+34	Pittsburgh (Marshall Avenue Interchange)
LR 1026 HOV St 25+ 45	North side of Veterans Bridge
LR 764, Sta. 582+06 WB	1/4 mile east of Liberty Bridge
McKees Rocks	At intersection of SR65 and Kleber Avenue
McKnight Road	Pittsburgh, Nelson Run Road
Mifflin Road	Near Glenwood Interchange
Mifflin Road	Near Glenwood Interchange
Mifflin Road	At Glenwood Interchange
Mifflin Road	Glenwood Interchange
Ohio River Blvd.	19-65 over Beaver Avenue turnaround
Ohio River Blvd.	TR19-65 SB over Ramp H
Ohio River Blvd.	Over Eckert Street
Parkway Center Ramp Road	0.4 mile southeast of SR 0121
Parkway Center SH	Over B&O RR and Brady Street
Parkway East	EB over Second Avenue

Owned and Maintained by PennDOT	
Bridge	Location/Description
Parkway East	I-376 WB over Brady Street
Parkway East	Second Avenue to Forbes Avenue
Parkway East	Over Forward Avenue
Parkway East SH	Frazier Street
Parkway West	Near Fort Pitt Garage
Parkway West	750 feet southwest of Fort Pitt Tunnels
Penn Lincoln Parkway	Bates Street Interchange
Penn Lincoln Parkway	Over SR 0019 SB
Penn Lincoln Parkway	Parkway East over Bates Street
Penn Lincoln Parkway	Saline Street Bridge
Perrysville Avenue	Over I-279
Ramp A Road	Ramp A, Fort Duquesne Bridge to Heinz Field
Ramp A Road	SR 837 NB to SR 885 SB
Ramp A Road	Grant Street Exit
Ramp A Road	Over Anderson Street
Ramp A Road	Off Ramp A to West Carson Street
Ramp A Road	Chateau Street Ramp A
Ramp A-D Road	Pittsburgh Ramp A-D
Ramp B Road	Ramp B to I-279 NB
Ramp B Road	Ramp B SB over Fontella Street
Ramp B Road	SR 837 NB to SR 885 NB
Ramp BU Road	Stanwix Street to Fort Pitt WB
Ramp C I-279 NB	Fort Pitt Bridge (NB) - Portal Bridge
Ramp C Road	TR 51 SB Ramp to Parkway West
Ramp C Road	Ramp C over Ramp F
Ramp C Road	Grant Street – Ramp C over Ramp D
Ramp C Road	Rt. 65 Ramp C SB/Beaver Avenue
Ramp D Road	Over Chateau Street N and S Ramp
Ramp D Road	Ramp D to Heinz Field
Ramp D Road, Exit 7B	Bates Street - Oakland Exit
Ramp E Road	Squirrel Hill Interchange
Ramp E Road	Brady Street SB On Ramp
Ramp E Road	Ramp E over Banksville Road NB
Ramp E SR 8151	0.1 mile south of Liberty Tunnel
Ramp F Road	Pittsburgh - Ramp F over G
Ramp F Road	Chateau Street to TR 65 NB

Owned and Maintained by PennDOT	
Bridge	Location/Description
Ramp F Road	Ramp F over Ramp D to 7th Avenue
Ramp F Road	Ramp F to Parkway East
Ramp F Road	Brady Street NB off Ramp
Ramp F SB	Ramp F SB to West End Bridge
Ramp G Road	228 EB over LR 1026
Ramp G Road	Ramp NB from 10th Street bypass
Ramp G Road	North of Veterans Bridge
Ramp G Road to Liberty Bridge	Just north of Liberty Bridge
Ramp H Road	1039 Ramp H NB to Fort Duquesne Bridge
Ramp H Road	Ramp H to Blvd. of Allies
Ramp H Road	NB I-579 to TR 28 NB
Ramp I Road	Ramp I-LR1021 over LR 805
Ramp J Road	Fort Duquesne Bridge to Fort Duquesne Blvd.
Ramp J Road	1021 Ramp J SB over SR 4003
Ramp K Road	Fort Duquesne South approach
Ramp L Road	Ramp from Liberty Bridge to 1026 NB
Ramp M Road	At Armstrong Tunnel
Ramp R Road	Over Brady Street/Oakland
Ramp S Road	LR 1021 HOV over McKnight
Ramp T Road	Ramp T to Parkway EB
Ramp U Road	Allies Blvd. Ramp to 764 WB
Ramp V Road	Heinz Field–Ramp V/TR 65 NB
Ramp V Road	Oakland Exit to Forbes
Ramp W Road	Near Heinz Field
Raymond E. Wilt Hwy	North of Veterans Bridge
R. D. Fleming (62nd Street) Bridge	Pittsburgh–Sharpsburg Line
RP B From Carson	Ramp B over West Carson Street
SR 19	150 feet south of West End Bridge
Saw Mill Run Blvd.	250 feet south of West End Circle
Saw Mill Run Blvd.	19 and 51 SB at West End Circle
Saw Mill Run Blvd.	125 feet south of Provost Road
Saw Mill Run Blvd.	250 feet southeast of SR 0088
Saw Mill Run Blvd.	At Whited Street
Saw Mill Run Blvd.	Near Bausman Street
Saw Mill Run Blvd.	0.1 mile south of Liberty Tunnel
Saw Mill Run Blvd.	At Warrington Avenue

Owned and Maintained by PennDOT	
Bridge	Location/Description
Shaler Street	1/4 mile northwest of SR 0279
Smithfield Street	Station Square
Smithfield Street	Smithfield Street Bridge
Smithfield Street	North approach span Smithfield Street
South Main Street	1200 feet west of West End Circle
SR 0019 SH	Ramp from Chateau Street to 19N
SR 0028 SH	LR 1040 WB over Madison Avenue
SR 0065 NB	1039 NB from Fort Duqusne Bridge
SR 0065 NB	TR 65 NB over Fontella Street
SR 0065 SB	1039 SB to Fort Duquesne Bridge
SR 0065 SB	TR 65 SB over Fontella Street
SR 0065 SH	Reedsdale ramp to Ridge Avenue
SR 0065 SH	NB over Allegheny Avenue
SR 0065 SH	1039 SB over Allegheny Avenue
SR 0279 SH	Portal Bridge/Point State Park
SR 0279 SH	Near Heinz Field
SR 0279 SH	Near Heinz Field
SR 0279 SH	Near Heinz Field
SR 0279 SH	1021 NB over 805 - Ramp J
SR 0279 SH	LR 1021 HOV over LR 805
SR 1005	Highland Park Bridge
SR 19 SH	North approach to West End Bridge
SR 279 SR	Under and parallel to I-279
SR 376 SH	Pittsburgh - Commercial Street
SR 376 WB, Ramp B	Ramp – Fort Pitt over Ramp A (F)
SR 51 Saw Mill Run	Near Edgebrook Avenue
SR 8095 (Ramp B)	At Intersection with Smithfield Street
Steubenville Pike	Thornburg Bridge
Thirty-first Street	Pittsburgh - 31st Street Bridge
TR 19 NB	350 feet west of Fort Pitt Tunnel
TR 51, SB	400 feet west of Fort Pitt Tunnel
Veterans Bridge	Veterans Bridge
Veterans Bridge Approach NB	South Approach to Veterans Bridge
Veterans Bridge Approach SB	I-579 SB off Veterans Bridge
Veterans Bridge Ramp B	Near Mellon Arena
Veterans Bridge Ramp J	South Approach to Veterans Bridge

Owned and Maintained by PennDOT	
Bridge	Location/Description
Webster Avenue	Webster Avenue over I-579
West Carson Street	1/2 mile northwest of Corliss Tunnel
West Carson Street	Pittsburgh at West End Circle
West End Bridge	West End Bridge
West End Circle (Route 837)	At south end of West End Bridge
West Liberty Avenue	At south end of Liberty Tunnel
Total Owned and Maintained by PennDOT: 186	

East Liberty Port Authority Busway pedestrian bridge.

Owned and Maintained by Port Authority of Allegheny County	
Bridge	Location/Description
B&O Railroad	East Busway/CSX RR
Brilliant Viaduct	Washington Blvd./N&S RR
Brookside Avenue	LRT/Brookside Avenue
Cape May Avenue	LRT/Cape May Avenue
Carson Street Flyover	Wabash HOV Flyover
Centre Avenue	East Busway/Centre Avenue
Corliss Tunnel Flyover	Corliss Tunnel/ N&S RR
Dahlem Street	East Busway/Dahlem Street

Owned and Maintained by Port Authority of Allegheny County	
Bridge	Location/Description
Duquense Incline	Duquesne Incline/N&S RR
Duquesne Incline Pedestrian	West Carson Street
East Liberty Ramp	East Liberty Bus Station
Edgebrook Avenue	South Busway/Edgebrook Avenue
Glenbury Road	LRT/Glenbury Road
McKinley Park	LRT/Bausman Street
McNeilly Road	LRT/McNeilly Road
Monongahela Incline	N&S RR and McArdle Roadway
Morange Road	West Busway/Morange Road
Negley Pedestrian	East Busway
Neville Ramp	East Busway/CSX RR
Norfolk & Western	South Busway
North Braddock Avenue	East Busway/North Braddock Avenue
North Homewood Avenue	East Busway/North Homewood Avenue
Oak Viaduct	LRT/Route 51
Oakwood Culvert	Oakwood Run
Panhandle	2nd Avenue and McKean Street
Panhandle Arlington	East Carson and Arlington Streets
Panhandle E. Carson	East Carson and McKean Streets
Pedestrian Overpass (#1)	East Busway
Pedestrian Overpass (#2)	East Busway
Penn Avenue	East Busway/N&S RR
Reflectorville Viaduct	LRT/Timberland Avenue
Saw Mill Run Blvd.	South Busway/Saw Mill Run Creek
Seventh Avenue	LRT Spur Line to Penn Station
South Bank Flyover	South Busway
South Hills Junction Flyover (#1)	LRT/Warrington Avenue
South Hills Junction Flyover (#2)	LRT/Warrington Avenue
26th Street Ramp	East Busway/N&S RR
28th Street	East Busway/Sassafrass Street
Wenzell Avenue	LRT/Wenzell Avenue
West Liberty Avenue	South Busway/West Liberty Avenue
West Liberty Avenue Ramp	South Busway/West Liberty Avenue (SB)
Whited Street	South Busway/Whited Street
Total Owned and Maintained by Port Authority of Allegheny County: 42	

A tired old railroad bridge on the North Side frames a dramatic view.

Railroads:

AVR	Allegheny Valley RR
BPRR	Buffalo & Pittsburgh RR
CSXT	CSX Transportation Inc
NSRC	Norfolk & Southern RR
POHC	Pittsburgh & Ohio Central RR
WE	Wheeling/Lake Erie RR

Owned and Maintained by Railroad Companies	
Bridge	Owner
Allegheny River Blvd.	AVR
Allegheny River Blvd.	AVR
Allegheny River Back Channel	CSXT
Allegheny River	33rd Street RR Bridge
Allegheny River	Fort Wayne RR Bridge
Allegheny River	Brilliant Branch RR
Allegheny Valley RR	BPRR
Arlington Avenue	NSRC

Owned and Maintained by Railroad Companies	
Bridge	Owner
Anderson Street	NSRC (AMTRAK)
Baldwin Road	NSRC
Becks Run Road	NSRC
Boundary Street	CSXT (AMTRAK)
Boundary Street	CSXT
Crane Avenue	WE
East Busway	BPRR
East Carson Street Ramp	NSRC
Eckert Street	NSRC (AMTRAK)
East Liberty Blvd.	NSRC (AMTRAK)
Edgebrook Avenue	WE
11th Street	NSRC (AMTRAK)
Federal Street	NSRC (AMTRAK)
Fifth Avenue	NSRC (AMTRAK)
Fifth Avenue	NSRC (AMTRAK)
Frankstown Road	AVR
Glen Mawr Street	CSXT
Glenbury Street	WE
Greenfield Avenue	AVR
Greenfield Avenue	CSXT (AMTRAK)
Greentree Road	WE
Haysglen Road	NSRC
Hamilton Avenue	AVR
Hamilton Avenue	AVR
Heinz Street	NSRC
Highland Drive	AVR
I-279 (Parkway West)	NSRC
I-279 (Parkway West)	WE
I-279 near Veterans Bridge	NSRC (AMTRAK)
I-279 near Veterans Bridge	NSRC (AMTRAK)
I-279 near Veterans Bridge	NSRC
Kelly Street	AVR
Laughlin Street	AVR
Liberty Avenue	BPRR

Owned and Maintained by Railroad Companies	
Bridge	Owner
Lincoln Avenue	AVR
Main Street	WE
McKnight Street	WE
Monongahela River	B&O RR Bridge-Glenwood
Mount Washington Tunnel	NSRC
North Dallas Avenue	NSRC (AMTRAK)
North Homewood Avenue	NSRC (AMTRAK)
Ohio River/Brunot Island	Ohio Connecting RR
Old Browns Hill Road	AMTRAK
Old J&L Steel yard	AVR
Penn Avenue	BPRR
16th Street	NSRC
South 18th Street	NSRC
South 21st Street	NSRC
South 22nd Street	NSRC
South 23rd Street	NSRC
South 24th Street	NSRC
South 26th Street	NSRC
South 27th Street	NSRC
Sandusky Street	NSRC (AMTRAK)
Smallman Street	BPRR
South Busway	WE
West Carson Street/Chartiers Creek	CSXT
West Carson/West End Circle	CSXT
West Liberty Avenue	WE
Whited Street	WE
Windgap Avenue/Chartiers Creek	POHC
(near) Woodruff Street	WE
Woodville Avenue	WE
Total Owned and Maintained by the Railroad Companies: 71	

REFERENCES AND SOURCES

Participants in the annual Race for the Cure swarm across the Panther Hollow Bridge in Oakland.

BOOKS AND MAGAZINES

Elkin, C. W. W. "The 1955 Historical Tour"; *Western Pennsylvania historical magazine*, No. 38, p. 135, 1955.

Gangewere, Robert J. *The Bridges of Pittsburgh and Allegheny County.* Pittsburgh, PA.: Science and Technology Department, Carnegie Library of Pittsburgh, 2001.

Herbertson, Elizabeth T. *Pittsburgh Bridges.* New York: Exposition Press, 1970.

Kidney, Walter C. *Pittsburgh Bridges: Architecture and Engineering.* Pittsburgh, PA: Pittsburgh History and Landmarks, 1999.

Lorant, Stephen. *Pittsburgh: The Story of an American City.* Lenox, MA: Authors Edition, Inc., 1964, 1975.

White, Joseph, and W. M. von Bernewitz. *The Bridges of Pittsburgh.* Crafton, PA: Cramer Printing and Publishing Company, 1928.

VIDEOS

Sebak, Rick. *Flying Off the Bridge to Nowhere!; and Other Tales of Pittsburgh Bridges.* Pittsburgh, PA: WQED, 1990.

INTERNET

Cridlebaugh, Bruce. *Bridges and Tunnels of Allegheny County and Pittsburgh;* www.pghbridges.com.

BRIDGE OWNERS

Allegheny County

City of Pittsburgh

Pennsylvania Department of Transportation (PennDOT)

Port Authority of Allegheny County

Various railroads

Opposite page: *Photo of author and photographer by Bill Wilson, City of Pittsburgh River Rescue Unit.*

AUTHOR AND PHOTOGRAPHER

On the back of the River Rescue Unit boat.

THE AUTHOR (RIGHT)

Bob Regan is a Visiting Professor at the University of Pittsburgh and a consultant specializing in Geographic Information Systems (GIS). His professional career includes senior level positions in the federal government, major corporations, and universities. His personal interests revolve around bicycling, and he manages, despite the Pittsburgh climate, to cover 2,000-3,000 miles a year doing so.

THE PHOTOGRAPHER (LEFT)

Tim Fabian is a professional photographer and president of Pro-Photo, Inc. (TimFabian.com). His work has been in numerous solo and group exhibitions and he is represented in several private and corporate collections as well as in magazines. When he isn't working on photography projects that interest him, lecturing, teaching, or serving as a juror for other artists, he can be found photographing Pittsburgh, his favorite subject.

Bob and Tim collaborated previously on *The Steps of Pittsburgh: Portrait of a City.* (ISBN 0-9711835-6-2). Published by The Local History Company, Pittsburgh, PA, 2004.

Detail from the Panther Hollow Bridge showing one of four panthers sculpted by Giuseppe Moretti

I N D E X

The Roberto Clemente Bridge.

*Page numbers in italics refer to maps and photographs; a "t"
after a page number refers to a table. Bridges shown only in
Appendix II: The Big List are not included in this index.*

175

McKnight Road Bridge at Nelson Run Road.

The Rachel Carson Bridge.